Faith in the Time of Covid 19

Archbishop Elpidophoros
of America

Greek Orthodox Archdiocese of America
8 East 79th Street, New York, 10075

www.goarch.org

ISBN: 978-1-58438-090-0

Faith in the Time of Covid 19

Archbishop Elpidophoros
of America

Homilies, Addresses & Messages
of His Eminence
Archbishop Elpidophoros of America

Great Lent – Pascha 2020

Index

Foreword

Your Eminence, Archbishop Elpidophoros of America, most honorable Exarch of the Atlantic and the Pacific Oceans, beloved brother and concelebrant of our Modesty in the Holy Spirit; may the grace, peace, and blessing of our Lord, God and Savior Jesus Christ be with you.

The word of the Church, the word of the life-giving Cross and the glorious Resurrection is the proclamation of the Gospel of the grace that came through the Incarnation of the pre-eternal Word of God and of the journey toward the Kingdom of the Eschaton, the "…new heavens and new earth in which righteousness dwells" (2 Peter 3:13).

The salvific message of the Church, which is always articulated in response to current circumstances and challenges, is a pastoral and loving intervention; it offers support, consolation, "truth"—and not mere assistance—, transfiguring our life, unveiling the depth of things, and opening the gate of paradise.

Beloved brother, this everlasting and always timely message regarding "the freedom to which Christ has set us free" (Gal. 5:1) is properly expressed in your texts, published in the present volume with the pertinent title "Faith in the Time of COVID-19." This edition includes homilies and messages from the troubling period of the pandemic, which created unprecedented problems in socio-economic life, but also in the life of the Church. These texts highlight the strength of faith in Christ, which enlightens the whole world, the radiance of the love which does not seek its own, and the comfort of the hope which does not disappoint us. In the life of the Christians, faith, love and hope consist in an undivided existential experience, which emanates the fragrance of the Resurrection.

The Church embraces the entirety of our existence, sanctifying our lives through its Eucharistic expression, through its sacraments, its spirituality, its pastoral ministry and its good witness in the world; the "liturgy after the Liturgy." We rejoice, because Your Eminence is vigilantly present and completely devoted to your flock in North America, living and preaching the Church as the "miracle of the new" in the world, and as a place of philanthropic sacrificial *diakonia*. In Christ, we received "all things" and we bear a responsibility to give "everything to all people," overcoming the hurdles and accomplishing our mission "through him who loved us" (Rm. 8:37).

The novel coronavirus pandemic has revealed the limits of human knowledge, and of our capacities and resilience. Nevertheless, it has also proclaimed that faith in the living God nourishes and reinforces the vital powers of man, fraternity, solidarity, and the desire for offer and sacrifice. It has also made manifest the value of the personal commitment of each one of us and of our common initiatives and actions. Self-centeredness diminishes our social responsibility, and favors the indifference toward the common good. The Holy and Great Council of the Orthodox Church (Crete, 2016) has rightly proclaimed that it is impossible to give answers to our serious existential problems and to the quest for meaning in our life "without a spiritual approach" (*Encyclical*, § 11).

In this spirit, we bless the current publication of your homilies and messages from the period of the *Triodion* and *Pentecostarion* in 2020, which coincides with the first stage of the pandemic, congratulating you for your affectionate interest in supporting and building up in Christ the faithful, and we unite our prayers with yours that the Savior of the world, Who is always with us and for us and "is the same yesterday and today and forever" (Heb. 13:8), the physician of our souls and bodies, the cause of all that is good, and the giver of every good and every perfect gift, may look down from heaven and speedily lead His people away from this crisis, strengthening Your Eminence to the pastoral care of your pious flock for the glory of His sacred name.

At the Ecumenical Patriarchate, January 12th, 2023
Your Eminence's beloved
brother in Christ,

† BARTHOLOMEW
Archbishop of Constantinople-New Rome
and Ecumenical Patriarch

Introduction

Beloved in Christ,

During the difficult times of the pandemic, and especially when we were forced to worship under great restrictions during the Days of Lent, Holy Week, and the very Pascha of the Lord, the messages in this collection were offered for the spiritual benefit of all.

I want to thank all of you, the People of the Church, for your faithfulness and support during these dark days, when even the light of the Resurrection had to be virtually passed from person to person. However, we know that the light of Christ burns most brightly within the human heart, which is the living temple of the Living God.

I pray that these reflections will continue to bless your lives, even as your gifts and offerings continue to bless others in their hour of need. We are one community in Christ, one Body of the Church, and just as we must care for every aspect of our physical body, we must show the same concern and love for every member of the Church, and indeed for every human person, for they too are made in the image and likeness of God.

I leave you with a simple request; that you take any good that you receive from these messages and share it with your neighbors in a spirit of love and genuine Christian concern. Love is the greatest gift that we can give, and the secret of the giving is the inexhaustible treasure-house of our Heavenly God who grants unto us eternal life and His great mercy.

With paternal love in Christ Jesus,

+Archbishop Elpidophoros of America

1

Kathara Deftera

March 2, 2020

HELLENIC COLLEGE HOLY CROSS
GREEK ORTHODOX SCHOOL OF THEOLOGY
BROOKLINE, MASSACHUSETTS

Beloved Children in the Lord,

Today is the Beginning of the Great and Holy Fast, the Monday of spiritual purity. I wish that I could be with all of you as you commence the race of the Forty Days that brings us to the holiest week of the year, but my responsibilities as Exarch of the Ecumenical Throne have called me away to South America, for the enthronement of the new Metropolitan Iosif.

But as the Holy Apostle Paul says:

For though I am absent in body, yet I am with you in spirit, rejoicing to see your good order and the firmness of your faith in Christ. (Colossians 2:5)

Indeed, our precious Σχολή is achieving good order and strengthening our Holy Orthodox Faith through all manner of initiatives, teaching, and above all, study. All members of the administration and faculty, and especially the students, are to be commended for their diligence, tenacity, and fidelity in the pursuit of the educational goals of the School.

Indeed, the Great and Holy Fast is also a course of study, but not of what others have said and taught. This education of intensive prayer, fasting, eleemosynary activity, and looking inward is an education of the self. A tithe, if you will, of your year, so that you may offer a realistic view of yourself to God, to each other, and to yourself.

The coursework is the remarkable collection of hymns, special services and readings that you all have the opportunity to experience every day here on the campus. But the work – the hard work of μετάνοια takes place within your own hearts, minds, and souls.

Μετάνοια, the combination of two words: μετά, and νοῦς, conveys much more than contrition, regret, or sorrow for one's failings. It is something like being in-between, of being in process, like the English word "metamorphosis." It is nothing less than the transformation – even the transfiguration – of your spiritual mind and heart.

The Holy Apostle Paul hints at this meaning in his Epistle to the Romans when he writes:

Καὶ μὴ συσχηματίζεσθαι τῷ αἰῶνι τούτῳ, ἀλλὰ μεταμορφοῦσθαι τῇ ἀνακαινίσει τοῦ νοὸς ὑμῶν....

And be not conformed to this world: but be transformed by the renewing of your mind....[1]

There is nothing passive about such a transformation, even though it occurs by grace and not by nature. Just feeling sorry for our sins is barely a beginning. We are called to work actively and intensively to transform our spiritual mind and heart: through prayer, through

2

reading and study, through acts of love, compassion, forgiveness, and mercy toward others.

Therefore, my beloved community of Hellenic College and Holy Cross, this Lent, make the most of the time. See that you walk circumspectly, redeeming the time that you spend in the Sacred Season.[2]

I pray that each and every one of you experiences the life-altering grace of God in a tangible and profound way, that you finish the course of the Fast to the best of your ability, and that you arrive at the Pascha of Lord with your hearts, minds, and spirits transfigured by salvific love that conquers death by His own death and grants us eternal life.

So be it. Γένοιτο. Amen.

---

1   Romans 12:2.
2   Cf. Ephesians 5:15,16.

2

First Salutations to the Theotokos

March 6, 2020

ARCHDIOCESAN CATHEDRAL OF THE HOLY TRINITY
NEW YORK, NEW YORK

Beloved and Dear Faithful,

Tonight, after the rigors and challenges of the very first days of the Holy Fast of the Forty Days, we arrive at this oasis in the desert that we call Great Lent. We have come to the first of the Salutations to the Theotokos and Ever-Virgin Mary, a fountain of spiritual refreshment and hearty and nourishing noetic meal of praise.

We sing to her: Χαῖρε! Χαῖρε Νύμφη Ἀνύμφευτε!

Rejoice! Rejoice Bride Unwedded!

We tell her stories – the story of her Annunciation and the Nativity of our Lord through the twenty-four stanzas composed by Saint Romanos the Melodist. With every encomium we offer her, we acclaim her virtues and we affirm her love, her power, and her advocacy for us before the Throne of God, where her Son is seated at the Right Hand.

Tonight, my beloved Christians, gathered here together in this Cathedral before her Holy Icon, we know that we are facing not only the challenge of the Fast, but also a challenge to the security of our physical health, the outbreak of the Coronavirus, named Covid-19.

We know that there are cases in our city, and that even though health and governmental authorities are doing all they can to address this issue, there are still possible risks to all of us.

That is why, especially in this season of the Fast, we go to the Mother of God with our prayers and supplications. As we chant in the fifth stanza, the one called "Epsilon":

Χαῖρε, ἄρουρα βλαστάνουσα εὐφορίαν οἰκτιρμῶν,
χαῖρε, τράπεζα βαστάζουσα εὐθηνίαν ἱλασμῶν.

Rejoice, Field bearing a bounty of compassions.
Rejoice, Table filled with an abundance of mercies.

We exalt the Virgin, not because she needs our praise, but because she is worthy to be magnified, as we chant throughout the year:

Ἄξιόν ἐστιν ὡς ἀληθῶς
Μακαρίζειν σὲ τὴν Θεοτόκον
Τὴν ἀειμακάριστον καὶ παναμώμητον
Καὶ Μητέρα τοῦ Θεοῦ ἡμῶν.

"It is truly worthy to bless you, the Theotokos, the ever-blessed and all-immaculate and Mother of our God!"

She is indeed a source of compassion and of mercy, because she not only shares our human nature with us, but she is the source of the human nature of her Son, Our Lord Jesus Christ. As the Apostle Paul says:

Ὅτε δὲ ἦλθε τὸ πλήρωμα τοῦ χρόνου, ἐξαπέστειλεν ὁ Θεὸς τὸν υἱὸν αὐτοῦ, γενόμενον ἐκ γυναικός....

But when the fullness of time came, God sent forth His Son, born of a woman....[3]

So just as we affirm in the Creed that the Lord Jesus is consubstantial with the Father – ὁμοούσιον τῷ Πατρί, in respect to His Divinity – He is also ὁμοούσιον τῇ Μητρί – consubstantial, of one essence, with His mother in respect to His humanity. The Holy Theotokos offered her human nature fully and completely to God at the moment of the Annunciation when she answered the Angel Gabriel:

Ἰδοὺ ἡ δούλη Κυρίου· γένοιτό μοι κατὰ τὸ ῥῆμά σου.

Behold the handmaid of the Lord; be it unto me according to your word.[4]

Therefore, the Virgin understands our every human predicament, our every challenge and threat ... even this outbreak of Covid-19. That is why we come to her in every Lenten season, and especially why we come to her tonight.

We ask for her intercessions.

We ask for her compassion.

We ask for her mercy.

That she would surround us with her protection, and bring to an end this outbreak and pandemic that afflicts our world.

7

And if we must endure, even to a cross of our own making, or of another's, we know that she will stand by us, even as she stood with Lord when He hung upon His Holy Cross.[5]

May we always know her "Field of compassions" and "Table of abundant mercies," and may we be blessed to complete the course of the Fast and arrive at the glorious Pascha of our Lord Jesus Christ.

Amen.

---

3   Galatians 4:4.
4   Luke 1:38.
5   John 19:25.

3

Sunday of Orthodoxy

March 8, 2020

Your Eminences and Graces,
Beloved Brothers and Sisters in Christ,

The joy of this First Sunday of the Holy Lent is multiplied by the presence of so many Hierarchs of our Holy Orthodox Faith within the Altar – united in faith, in brotherhood, in solidarity of commitment, and in prayer. I am so very pleased that our Serbian, Ukrainian, Georgian, Romanian, Carpatho-Russian and OCA friends decided to choose the unity of the faith today – to choose the spiritual fraternity and be with us here in our Archdiocesan Cathedral, in which the episcopacy of our Holy Archdiocese is so well represented by the Metropolitan of Atlanta, our beloved brother Alexios, and the Chief Secretary of our Eparchial Synod, our beloved brother Apostolos.

Allow me, if you will, to name each of these Hierarchs:

Metropolitan Anthony and Archbishop Daniel of the Ukrainian Church of the United States, Ecumenical Patriarchate.

Metropolitan Gregory of the Carpatho-Russian Diocese of the Ecumenical Patriarchate.

Archbishop Michael and Bishop Alexis of the OCA.

Bishop Irinej of the Serbian Orthodox Church, whose most esteemed Patriarch visited our Holy Archdiocese this past week.

Bishop Saba of the Georgian Orthodox Church.

Bishop Ierotheos of the Patriarchal Monastery of Saint Irene Chrysovolantou.

And last but certainly not least, Father Ioan Cosam representing the Romanian Diocese of the OCA.

All of these honorable clergy, together with the those of our Cathedral and Archdiocese, are gathered on this First Sunday of the Holy Fast to bear witness to the essential unity and integrity of what it means to be an Orthodox Christian.

Yes, we differ in jurisdiction; we differ in ethnic background; we differ in native language; we differ in customs. But the Faith that we confess is in the One, Holy, Catholic, and Apostolic Church! We believe and we confess the same Nicene-Constantinopolitan Creed. We share in the Same Eucharistic Meal – the Mystical Supper of the Lord. And we all look forward to the Same Glorious Resurrection of our God in His Holy Pascha.

Being an Orthodox Christian is a wonderful gift – whether you were born into an Orthodox family or you chose to become Orthodox at some point in your life. We have an inexhaustible supply of treasures from around the world. Different ways of chanting, of celebrating, of painting holy icons, but all of them are focused on the one reality of our salvation which comes about through the grace of the Holy Trinity: the pre-eternal will of the Father, the sacrifice from the foundation of the world of the Son, and the continuous sanctifying operation of the Holy Spirit.

Sometimes, I think that we get too caught up in our differences and forget that we are the same family. As the Ecumenical Patriarch has reminded us so many times: we are not a confederation of churches but we are the Church! One family, one Γένος, one Ἐκκλησία – which means, as you know: "The Assembly of Those who are Called Forth."

Well then, if we have all been called forth, what have we been called to do? What is our purpose, our mission? To preach, teach, and live the Gospel of our Lord Jesus Christ. It is no accident that we gathered together today in this Cathedral. We are here for a purpose, to find our way to live in the fellowship of the Holy Spirit, by the grace of our Lord Jesus Christ, in the love of God the Father.

We manifest our purpose here in the Divine Liturgy, sharing in the Most Holy Body and Blood of our Lord, and seeing in each other the fullness of God's love for each and every one. If we say we love God, then we must love each other. If we say that we come to the Chalice for forgiveness and mercy, then we must offer forgiveness and mercy to each other as God does, unconditionally.

This is not an easy way to live. It requires attention, interior vigilance, discipline, knowledge, faith, hope, and above all, love. And to help guide us to all these is today's Gospel reading. A small detail may illuminate it for you. The Lord said to Nathanael:

Ὄντα ὑπὸ τὴν συκῆν εἶδόν σε!

While you were sitting beneath the fig tree, I saw you![6]

The fig tree is an image of community in the New Testament, sometimes specific to the Synagogue, where the Lord learned as a child and taught in word and deed after His revelation to Israel. We can see in it an image of our communities as well. Some are full of fruit, some are bereft of anything to harvest, and some are withering up. And we are all sitting in them, like Nathanael beneath the fig tree where the Lord saw him.

And just like Nathanael, the Lord sees us as well, and knows our hearts, knows our intentions, and our reasons for being here today. Maybe someone brought you today into the presence of the Christ, like Philip brought Nathanael. Maybe you wandered in out of habit. Maybe you are searching for something deeper. The Good News, the Gospel tells us that the Lord already knows everything about us that there is to know. What a relief! We don't have to explain ourselves to Him. We just have to be willing to encounter Him, to follow Him, and to live the life He offers us.

Today in our Cathedral, you all have witnessed the fruits of this life, how good and joyous it can be to dwell in unity with brothers and sisters, with the living icons of God.[7] We are not gathered by accident. God sees us even at this very moment. May we always be found in the Church in such unity and peace. Amen!

---

6   John 1:49.

7   Cf. Psalm 133:1.

4

Second Salutations to the Theotokos

March 13, 2020

Beloved and Dear Faithful,

Tonight we sing to the Virgin:

Χαῖρε, ἀοράτων ἐχθρῶν ἀμυντήριον!

Rejoice, Bulwark against invisible foes!

Could there be a more fitting time to give this praise to the Theotokos and invoke her prayers and intercessions for our lives?

As happy as I am to be here at Saint Peter's this evening, the truth is that I was scheduled to be in New Rochelle at Holy Trinity. But you all know that New Rochelle has become an epicenter of the local outbreak, and gatherings of all kinds have been cancelled by the State government.

The threat of the Coronavirus, Covid-19, is a real and present danger in our country. And we do not know how this pandemic will end.

The Archdiocese, as a community of believers, has taken measures that we deem prudent and rational, consistent with science and consistent with our Faith, in order to decrease the possibility of our parishes becoming points of transmission of the disease.

We know that there is a quality to our challenges that goes beyond what is visible to the eye. As St. Paul states in his letter to the Ephesians:

Οὐκ ἔστιν ἡμῖν ἡ πάλη πρὸς αἷμα καὶ σάρκα, ἀλλὰ πρὸς τὰς ἀρχάς, πρὸς τὰς ἐξουσίας, πρὸς τοὺς κοσμοκράτορας τοῦ σκότους τοῦ αἰῶνος τούτου, πρὸς τὰ πνευματικὰ τῆς πονηρίας ἐν τοῖς ἐπουρανίοις.

We wrestle not against flesh and blood, but against principalities, against powers, against the rulers of the darkness of this world, against spiritual wickedness in high places.[8]

Therefore, knowing that our struggle is against more than what is subject to flesh and blood, we invoke our Heavenly Champion and we chant:

Τῇ ὑπερμάχῳ στρατηγῷ τὰ νικητήρια,
ὡς λυτρωθεῖσα τῶν δεινῶν εὐχαριστήρια,
ἀναγράφω σοι ἡ πόλις σου, Θεοτόκε·
ἀλλ' ὡς ἔχουσα τὸ κράτος ἀπροσμάχητον,
ἐκ παντοίων με κινδύνων ἐλευθέρωσον,
ἵνα κράζω σοί· Χαῖρε Νύμφη ἀνύμφευτε.

To You the Champion, we your City dedicate
a feast of victory and of thanksgiving,
as ones rescued out of sufferings, O Theotokos.
But as you are one with might that is invincible,

from all dangers that can be deliver us,
that we may cry to you:
Rejoice, Bride unwedded!

* * *

This magnificent hymn is regarded by many to have been composed by the Patriarch Germanos in the year 718, in thanksgiving for the rescue of the Queen of Cities, our beloved Constantinople, from an overwhelming attack by sea. It is said that the Patriarch gathered the faithful in the Agia Sophia and that these hymns were chanted throughout the entire night – all four Stanzas of the Kontakion of Saint Romanos the Melodist – until the victory was won. And they chanted them all night long standing! Thus the Kontakion became known as the Ἀκάθιστος, or "Akathist" – the hymn of "not sitting."

Therefore, we also, gathered together in this wonderful Church of the Holy Trinity, implore the Most Holy Theotokos and Ever-Virgin Mary to grant us her protection, her mercies, her fervent defense against every seen and unseen enemy to our Church, our homes, our families, our bodies and our souls.

We take every precaution that is reasonable and scientifically valid, and at the same time, we affirm our miraculous God Who transcends matter, space, and time. This is a middle way, a way that goes to neither an extreme on the right or the left, as the Prophet Moses exhorts.[9] We know that in the Mysteries of our Church, God is with us. His presence is real, and the faith that we need to apprehend His presence is nothing else than that of the young Virgin who assented to the word of the Angel. With her rational mind, she was unable to master the miracle that was about to be wrought in her, but she trusted in the Lord, and remember, my friends, trust is just another word for faith, for πίστις.

So take courage, my beloved Christians. Hold fast to your faith, your hope, and your love. The Holy Virgin will honor you and spread her loving embrace over you and your families, for she is the Πλατυτέρα τῶν Οὐρανῶν, the "One More Spacious than the Heavens." There is room for everyone in her loving arms. She is truly the Mother of us all.

Through her prayers may we all complete these days of the Great Lent and attain the Holy Resurrection of our Lord Jesus Christ.

Amen.

---

8   Ephesians 6:12.
9   Deuteronomy 5:32.

5

Archdiocese District Clergy-Laity Address

March 14, 2020

SAINT NICHOLAS GREEK ORTHODOX CHURCH
FLUSHING, NEW YORK

Your Grace,
Reverend Fathers and Presbyteras,
Delegates to the Clergy Laity Assembly,
Brothers and Sisters in Christ,

Here, at the end of the second week of the Holy and Great Lent, we find ourselves gathered as one family in Christ to deliberate as Clergy and Laity together. And we have many challenges ahead, not the least of which is dealing with the outbreak of the Coronavirus, Covid-19, in a theologically appropriate and scientifically responsible manner. This contagion has yet to relent in our country and our world, and as leaders in our communities, we are all bound to act and to speak in ways that affirm our Faith and assure our Faithful. If there are further questions beyond those addressed in the Encyclical and Pastoral Guidelines, the Chancellor and your local Vicars will be able to assist you and your parishes. We must be confident in the Lord our

God, as well as vigilant in all our decisions. People will look to you, the leadership of the parishes, as well as to us, for prudent advice and guidance. We must be ready to answer clearly, without hesitation.

As the Holy Scripture says:

Οὐ γὰρ ἔδωκεν ἡμῖν ὁ Θεὸς Πνεῦμα δειλίας, ἀλλὰ δυνάμεως καὶ ἀγάπης καὶ σωφρονισμοῦ.

For God has not given to us a spirit of cowardice; but one of power, and of love, and of moderation.[10]

We must speak to the people as did the Lord,[11] with love and compassion, and with moderation and prudence.

This is one of the blessings of having the new system of Vicars already in place throughout the Direct Archdiocesan District. We can be more responsive and pay more attention to all of your needs, not only questions about the Coronavirus. The Vicars are in constant communication with the Chancellor and my office, so if there are questions or problems, you should not hesitate to call on them.

We see how just yesterday, the Annual Greek Independence Parade was cancelled as was the Annual Celebration of Greek Independence at the White House which was scheduled for March 18th. As for the visit of His All-Holiness in May, I want you to know that we are monitoring the situation daily – with the White House, with the State Department, and with the Department of Health and Human Services. We will let you know as soon as we have news that impacts on the trip.

Although I am personally honored that he would come to America during the first anniversary of my election as Archbishop, I am utterly convinced that the most important venue of the Ecumenical Patriarch's visit will be that to the newly restarted construction at

Ground Zero and the future Saint Nicholas Church and National Shrine. We are removing the plastic coverings on April 2nd, and if we are able to hold a public gathering, I urge all of you to bring as many of your faithful as possible to Ground Zero on that day to bear witness to the Nation of the renewed construction of our National Shrine.

I know there are doubters in our community, those who seek out every opportunity to criticize. But I can tell you this: in just two days, I will depart for Minnesota to visit the company that is fabricating the curtain wall of the Church. Just because you may not see construction cranes surrounding 130 Liberty Street at this time, don't think that nothing is happening. In fact, we are pushing ahead full steam with work on Saint Nicholas. And before this Holy Week, you will see construction activity re-commence at the site, two and one half years after it came to an abrupt and embarrassing halt.

Believe me, this has not been an easy recovery, with all of the financial challenges we inherited at both the Archdiocese and the Theological School. The stoppage of work at Ground Zero has had enormous costs associated with it, costs that were unforeseen and unexpected. But with the help and confidence of our laypeople – many of them here in this room today, we have set the ship of the Archdiocese on the right course and we are nearer to our goal than, as the Apostle says, when we first believed.[12]

Over 40 million dollars has been donated since the beginning of the year, and we are well on our way to finishing and opening the Saint Nicholas Church and National Shrine at the rebuilt World Trade Center. Soon, on September 11, 2021 – the bicentennial year of Greek Independence, we will take our place with all the magnificent structures that adorn Ground Zero.

But we will be the only House of Worship on the Site, because we were the only House of Worship destroyed on 9/11. Our presence at

Ground Zero is an enormous privilege and responsibility of which we must be worthy, and the parishes of the Direct Archdiocesan District – the sister parishes of the National Shrine – have an important role to play as we develop ministries around the Shrine.

Finally, I wish to express to all of you, priests and lay leaders alike, my deep appreciation and gratitude for your incredible service to our communities, and especially to me during my first year of ministry here in America.

Your faith, your dedication, your hard work are truly inspiring and I want you to know that even as the Lord knows every sparrow,[13] I also know and am deeply grateful for your every effort on behalf of the DAD and our Church. I am particularly gratified that we are doing more and more for our youth, and this is something that cannot ever cease. Our youth are not only our future, they are our present as well!

Therefore, may the Lord continue to bless you and your families throughout the remainder of this Great and Holy Lent, keep all of us safe and healthy through this crisis, and grant that you attain His Holy Resurrection on the sacred night of the Holy Pascha!

---

10   II Timothy 1:7.
11   Cf. Matthew 7:29.
12   Cf. Romans 13:11.
13   Cf. Matthew 10:29.

6

⟨━◆━◆━◆━◆━◆━◆━⟩

Exhortation at the Conclusion
of the Divine Liturgy

The Second Sunday of the Great Lent

March 15, 2020

GREEK ORTHODOX CHURCH OF OUR SAVIOR
RYE, NEW YORK

Dear Brothers and Sisters in Christ,

These are not easy times that we are living in. There are tremendous threats to our way of life from the appearance of the Coronavirus around the world. While we are gathered together in this magnificent Church of our Savior in Rye, New York, the services are being broadcast in Greece and we are joined in spirit with them, for they are also under the same conditions.

In this time of pandemic, we are called to walk in a middle path, in a harmony and balance between the principles of our Faith and the facts of science.

As our Holy Ecumenical Patriarchate has stated:

It is considered self-evident that faith in God, as transcendence and not as the abolition of human reason, along with prayer, strengthen the spiritual battle of every Christian. Therefore, the Mother Church of Constantinople urges its spiritual children throughout the world to intensify their petitions so that, strengthened and illumined by God, this contemporary tribulation may be overcome.

The gift of human reason is as precious as the gift of faith. Together, they bring us to the very best of our humanity. Reason allows us to take precautions, have a measured and appropriate response that avoids panic, and uses the tools of science to alleviate suffering.

Faith allows us to be compassionate, to be loving and concerned for the most vulnerable among us, and take courage as the Lord encourages us with a single word: Θαρσεῖτε!

My beloved Christians, we are facing difficulties, but we are not only facing them together. We are facing them with God by our side. Take courage! Θαρσεῖτε! He overcame the world,[14] and we will overcome this pandemic, by the glory of His Holy Name, and for the sake of our world, our Nation, our communities, our families, and all those we love.

---

14 Cf. John 16:33.

7

Third Salutations to the Theotokos

March 20, 2020

SAINTS CONSTANTINE AND HELEN GREEK ORTHODOX CHURCH
JACKSON HEIGHTS, NEW YORK

Beloved and Dear Faithful,
Brothers and Sisters in Christ,

I address all of you this evening through the marvel of technology that allows us to be connected in real time, during this worldwide Covid-19 Pandemic. We cannot deny that there is a new reality that we must all face, and with faith, hope, and love, we will meet every challenge.

This broadcast is part of what is called "social distancing," a way for us to keep our own health safe and to protect the health of others. It is why the Holy Mother and Great Church of Christ wisely called for all Her communities to refrain from assembling for Divine Services, at least through the end of this month.

Rather, we are celebrating in a minimal way, with few bodies, but with many spirits. This "social distance" does not mean that we are spiritually apart. In fact, not even the broadcast of this service can do what our God can do – bring us together into communion in the spirit, even if temporarily we cannot constitute a community in the body.

We chanted the Third Stanza of the Salutations tonight in this wonderful Church of Saints Constantine and Helen in Jackson Heights, New York. And just as in this beautiful church we are surrounded by the icons, the Saints, the Angels and the Mother of God herself, I say to all of you: We are surrounded by you as well.

We are surrounded by your love.

We are surrounded by your faithfulness.

We are surrounded by your deep yearning to be with us at this holy time and in this holy place.

But please understand this, you are sanctified in your homes as you are sanctified here. You are part of the *Ekklesia* in your homes as you are part of the *Ekklesia* here.

Keep in mind these comforting words of Saint Paul:

Πέπεισμαι γὰρ ὅτι οὔτε θάνατος οὔτε ζωὴ οὔτε ἄγγελοι οὔτε ἀρχαὶ οὔτε δυνάμεις οὔτε ἐνεστῶτα οὔτε μέλλοντα οὔτε ὕψωμα οὔτε βάθος οὔτε τις κτίσις ἑτέρα δυνήσεται ἡμᾶς χωρίσαι ἀπὸ τῆς ἀγάπης τοῦ Θεοῦ τῆς ἐν Χριστῷ Ἰησοῦ τῷ Κυρίῳ ἡμῶν.

For I am convinced that neither death nor life, nor Angels, nor Principalities nor Powers, nor things present, nor things future, nor height, nor depth, nor any other created thing, will be able to separate us from the love of God that is in Christ Jesus, our Lord![15]

Nothing can separate us from the love of God! And if you need proof of this, we have two thousand continuous years of the intercessions of His Holy Mother, who stands with us in our hour of need.

24

A mother's love may be the greatest love a human can experience, because it is the mother who gives of her very body to conceive and nurture us, while we are formed in the womb.

It is the mother's love that brings us forth into this world, though she must endure much pain and labor to do so. How many of you know that the only description of the Passion and the terrible Sacrifice of the Cross that our Lord Jesus Christ ever gave to His Disciple is of a woman giving birth? As He Himself says in the Gospel of John:

Ἡ γυνὴ ὅταν τίκτῃ, λύπην ἔχει, ὅτι ἦλθεν ἡ ὥρα αὐτῆς· ὅταν δὲ γεννήσῃ τὸ παιδίον, οὐκέτι μνημονεύει τῆς θλίψεως διὰ τὴν χαρὰν ὅτι ἐγεννήθη ἄνθρωπος εἰς τὸν κόσμον.

When a woman is in labor, she has pain because her time has come. But when she has brought forth the child, she no longer remembers her distress because of her joy that a human being is born into the world.[16]

And it is the mother's love that feeds us from her own body, even as the Lord suckled at his Holy Mother's breast and was nourished thereby.

And so, my friends, we are so very blessed to have His Holy Mother with us in prayer and supplication this evening and in every day and hour. As the pious woman cried aloud:

Μακαρία ἡ κοιλία ἡ βαστάσασά σε καὶ μαστοὶ οὓς ἐθήλασας.

Blessed is the womb that gave birth to You, and the breasts that You suckled![17]

Let us run to our Mother, the Mother of God and Ever-Virgin Mary, with our cares, our anxieties, our fears, and as a loving mother who dries the eyes of her tear-laden child, she will comfort us in the deep places of our hearts and minds. She will strengthen us with her love, which is the love of our Holy Mother Church, our Holy Ecumenical Patriarchate, and our Holy Archdiocese of America for all the Faithful and for the whole world.

Amen.

---

15   Romans 8:38,39.
16   John 16:21.
17   Luke 11:27.

8

Fourth Salutations to the Theotokos

March 27, 2020

HOLY TRINITY GREEK ORTHODOX CHURCH
HICKSVILLE, NEW YORK

Beloved and Dear Faithful,

Tonight we are gathered across the region and the Nation, not in our Church temple, but in our homes, in order to chant this Fourth Stanza of the Salutations to the Theotokos. In this time of the global pandemic, we are taking every necessary step to flatten the curve of the rate of infection, to protect both the Faithful and the Clergy.

But we cannot, and we will not, forsake our commitment to live the liturgical life of the Church during these very difficult days.

That is why I have traveled to Hicksville, New York, to this wonderful parish of the Holy Trinity, to chant and praise the name of the Virgin with you. Whether you are live-streaming this service, or are simply in the privacy of your personal prayers because of the hardships we are facing during this very serious public health crisis, we are still the Church, and the Theotokos is still our Mother!

As we chanted tonight:

Χαῖρε, τῆς Ἐκκλησίας ὁ ἀσάλευτος πύργος,
Χαῖρε, τῆς Βασιλείας τὸ ἀπόρθητον τεῖχος.

Rejoice, unshakeable Tower of the Church,
Rejoice, fortified Bulwark of the Kingdom!

The Theotokos is the greatest protector of the Church, for in her defense of the Church, she is defending the Body of her child, for the Ekklesia is the Body of Christ.

Think what a mother would give for her child – anything! There is nothing that a mother would not do, not give, not sacrifice for her child.

So tonight, in the midst of this worldwide crisis,
in the midst of fear and anxiety,
of isolation and loneliness,
of pain and for many deep loss,
we cry out to the Mother of God who is also our Heavenly Mother:

Ὦ πανύμνητε Μῆτερ, ἡ τεκοῦσα τὸν πάντων ἁγίων, ἁγιώτατον
Λόγον· δεξαμένη γὰρ τὴν νῦν προσφοράν, ἀπὸ πάσης ῥῦσαι συμφορᾶς
ἅπαντας, καὶ τῆς μελλούσης λύτρωσαι κολάσεως, τοὺς σοὶ βοῶντας·
Ἀλληλούια.

O All-hymned Mother, who did bear the Word more holy than all
the Saints, receive now our offering, and rescue us all from every
calamity – especially this present pandemic, and redeem us from
any future torment as we cry to you: Alleluia!

This is the very last prayer of the Akathist Hymn, one that we repeat with yearning and intensity. Our appeal is all the more urgent because we are living in very calamitous times.

Our cry unto Heaven is sincere, spiritual, and efficacious. It is not just a psychological release from the stress we are enduring.

This magnificent poem that we call the Akathist Hymn is our way of communicating to the Mother of God, and asking for her intercessions with her Son and God, for her Son's little brothers and sisters – that's us – who are still on this earth.

The earth suffers, and we suffer with it. But the Mother of God suffered too:

when she lost her Son in the Temple during his twelfth Passover;

when she lost her Son on the Cross in only His thirty-third year of earthly life.

But she found Him again through His glorious Resurrection, and we too shall be found again in safety and in health, when we have passed through this difficult season of sickness.

My brothers and sisters, let us hold fast to the Mother of God, and run to her for consolation, comfort and healing.

And let us cry out to her: Alleluia!

Amen.

9

Archdiocese Presbyters Council
Virtual Town Hall

March 28, 2020

ARCHDIOCESE HEADQUARTERS
NEW YORK, NEW YORK

Beloved Brothers in the Lord,

I greet each and every one of you in the love of Christ and with my deep appreciation for all that you are doing for the Faithful during this global pandemic. We have all been caught off guard and I know that you are all doing your best to keep your vital ministries going in every way possible.

The truth is no one was prepared for the consequences of such a rapid and widespread transmission of the Covid-19 virus. Our civil authorities and our healthcare system are still reeling from trying to catch up with the virus, and we do not know for certain whether we have flattened the curve of the rate of infection. Furthermore, each area of the country is being differently affected, and will have differing regulations from region to region. So we are in a time that needs our utmost attention.

But I also know that through the grace of God, with the intercessions of His Holy Mother and all the Saints, we will get through this crisis. This is a time that challenges our faith, but our faithful will look to us to be their support and show them the way.

Therefore, I counsel all of us to lean upon the Lord, as it says in the Psalm:

The Lord is my foundation, and my refuge, and my deliverer. My God is my helper, and I will hope in Him.... [18]

The greatest service that you can offer to your parishioners right now is to give them the encouragement to make it through another day with hope and expectation for the future.

And this is not so easy. We all began the year with many high hopes and many plans, and today, we need to be prepared and flexible in our thinking, so that rather than react to conditions, we can respond in a way that affirms our leadership to the Faithful. They look to us when we are not looking. They listen to us, and they read our signals. We must pay extra care to how we shepherd the Flock of Christ during this crisis.

Let me say a few words about how we are conducting the Divine Services right now. We have taken extraordinary measures – and I do mean the restrictions about limiting our public assemblies. But never forget, the Ekklesia extends far beyond the four walls of any church building. We are celebrating the Divine Liturgy for the life of the world, and whether your service is live-streamed or not, it is vital that it take place.

The Divine Liturgy is wherever two or three are gathered in His Holy Name,[19] and where the worship of God is, as the Lord commands, "in spirit and in truth."[20] If you are live-streaming, please show great care with how your service is shown on video. Better not to present the Liturgy in a format with poor audio and bad camera angles than to broadcast it at all.

Remember, the Divine Service is not a show; it is worship, and the Faithful are edified just knowing that the Liturgy of the Church continues. They will pray and chant, light candles and burn incense, venerate icons and even relics in their own homes.

By a strange twist of fate, this restricted season is an opportunity for them to reinvigorate their spiritual lives in the context of their homes, and this is certainly a good outcome from a bad situation. Moreover, this season of fasting from the Divine Services is creating the holy desire for the Banquet of the Liturgy. The faithful will be even more hungry for the tangible experience of worship once the danger has passed. In the meanwhile, our conduct as clergy, and how we bring the value of our ministry to the faithful, is more important than ever.

Be a model pastor. Ask your faithful for their needs; ask them for names to pray for, and assure them of your prayers for them. Your parishioners need to know that you are commemorating all of them by name in every *Proskomide*, aloud and with a particle for each name. They need you to communicate with them regularly and frequently. Reach out personally across all communication platforms, from the traditional telephone, to digital on social media and video conferencing.

Make home visits and bring Holy Communion to them as they request, and offer the Sacrament, even if they do not request. The Holy Eucharist, as our Ecumenical Patriarchate noted just two weeks ago in an official Communiqué,[21] is the "antidote to death," and we affirm that the Most Holy Body and the Most Precious Blood of our Lord Jesus Christ is a source of only life, and eternal life at that! And we affirm that the traditional way of receiving the Eucharist is not a vector for disease of any kind. Please do not get into scholastic discussions about what aspect of which is holy. Leave such as this to the Scribes and Pharisees who want to be right about everything.

We know that if the living icon of God, the human being, can transmit the virus, then there will be cases of transmission within the confines of the Church. This is ultimately the purpose of restricting attendance at this time.

But this does not mean that we alter, as the Lord says: ἰῶτα ἓν ἢ μία κεραία – "not a iota, not a dot,"[22] of our Holy Orthodox Faith. We maintain without pause or interruption the teaching of the Church, and, as our Mother Church counsels us, we remain "firm in the Orthodox teaching regarding the Holy Eucharist."[23]

In addition to our attention to the Divine Services and the Sacramental needs of our parishioners, we are also obligated to think outside the box for our pastoral ministry. Just the other day, our Three Hierarchs Church in Brooklyn did a beautiful service to its local neighborhood and community. Father Pappas enlisted a local parishioner who was a florist, and the next thing you know there was a magnificent cross of flowers on the Church steps with a sign that read: "Take a flower for hope." What a beautiful way to witness to the Gospel, and to do so observing both all health precautions and all legal restrictions.

This kind of initiative and out of the box thinking is to be commended, and it is effective in maintaining the presence of the Church in a tangible and physical way.

But there is also the virtual method of having "touch points" for your parishioners. Over the coming days, the Archdiocese will be providing you a "digital tool box" that will cover needs ranging from online donations to parish "streaming kits," to keep your parish running both financially and liturgically.

In this time of restricted movement – and we do not yet know how long these restrictions will remain in force, for they will surely differ from locality to locality, we must apply ourselves with innovation and ingenuity.

There is a presentation that the APC will make to each and every one of you that will have suggestions, recommendations, and information to help you through this crisis of applicable ministry in a time of restricted freedom of assembly.

Please makes sure that you work in concert with the guidance of our Holy Mother Church the Ecumenical Patriarchate and your local Metropolitan and their staff. This is a crisis that we can come through with even greater spiritual vitality than before, because even though the flesh is indeed weak, our spirits are willing, ready and able.

Two final words...

The first concerns Holy Week and Pascha. We do not yet know whether we shall be able to celebrate with the Assembly of the Faithful, and we are preparing, if necessary, recommendations for how to observe this most sacred Week of the year without the participation of your parishioners. These guidelines will come as suggestions so that your people do not feel utterly left out of the Holy Services.

Second, the much-anticipated Apostolic Visit of His All-Holiness to America is in doubt as I speak, not only because venues will be closed off and others may be cancelled, but because we have to take into consideration the time it will take to restore social confidence after the crisis has passed.

My brothers in Christ, we are experiencing a worldwide plague from which recovery in our physical, social, psychological, emotional, and financial lives has yet to begin.

What we can do now is to concentrate on our spiritual recovery, and give the blessed assurance to our people – the People of God –

that the Church will always be there for them, and that with faith, hope, and the love of God, we will overcome, we will see brighter days, and the Resurrection will triumph over all.

---

18   Psalm 17:1,2 (LXX).
19   Cf. Matthew 18:20.
20   John 4:24.
21   March 11, 2020.
22   Matthew 5:18.
23   Communiqué of the Holy and Sacred Synod, March 11, 2020.

10

◆━◉━◉━◉━◉━◆

Fourth Sunday of Lent

March 29, 2020

Beloved Brothers and Sisters in Christ,

I have traveled today from the Church Headquarters in Manhattan to this amazing parish on Staten Island, the Holy Trinity-Saint Nicholas Greek Orthodox Church, in order to celebrate the Divine Liturgy with you – in the Spirit, through prayer, and through the medium of live-streaming.

We are still in a period of tremendous restriction, all for the sake of the health of our fellow citizens and our own health as well. My hope is that we will seize the opportunity that is literally being forced upon us, to become more altruistic, more compassionate toward others, more patient, and indeed more faithful.

I know that this is not easy. Many of us are facing serious consequences:

That affect our health,
That affect our families,
That affect our friends,
They affect our finances,
They affect our future.

As that great American Revolutionary Thomas Paine said, "These are the times that try men's souls."[24] In these days of anxiety and worry, we are not unlike the father of the boy that we hear of in today's Gospel reading, who came to our Lord Jesus Christ, begging Him to heal his son.

His son was in danger. Our lives are in danger. The man went to the Apostles for help, and we go to the Saints for help.

But in the moment when no results had happened, and the Lord challenged this father's faith, this man, who was already on his knees before Christ, exclaimed with the pain of his soul:

Πιστεύω, Κύριε· βοήθει μου τῇ ἀπιστίᾳ!

I believe, Lord! Help my unbelief![25]

My beloved friends, this is where we are right now. We do believe in God. We do trust that He is a Loving and Merciful God. We do confess that the arc of His inscrutable will ultimately bend toward our benefit and to the good of all.

But we still have our doubts in our minds and pain in our hearts. We look around and we see the world paralyzed by this pandemic. We feel the collapse of many systems of our world upon which we have always depended: employment, finance, health, and even simple things like going to the grocery store or a pharmacy.

This is where we find ourselves, just like the father of this boy. Things are falling apart around us, and we are on our knees before the Lord.

In this moment, it is no sin to have a mind clouded with doubt and anxiety. It makes us no less Christian to question, and to wonder. It makes us human.

But in the fullness of our humanity, let us not despair. Let us not lose every hope. Let us cry with the father of this child:

Πιστεύω, Κύριε· βοήθει μου τῇ ἀπιστίᾳ!

I believe, Lord! Help my unbelief![26]

It is God Himself Who is the source of our faith, and He is able to increase our confidence in Him, when we create space within ourselves to accept Him. As the Psalmist says:

Ὁδὸν ἐντολῶν σου ἔδραμον, ὅταν ἐπλάτυνας τὴν καρδίαν μου.

I have run the way of Your commandments, when You have enlarged my heart.[27]

Therefore, let us open our hearts to God, and seek his will, and obey His commandments, the greatest of which is to love one another.[28] And it shall be for us as the saint we commemorate this day, Saint John of Ladder, says:

"The power of love is in hope, because by hope we await the reward of love."[29]

Amen.

---

24   Thomas Paine, The American Crisis, December 19, 1776.
25   Mark 9:24.
26   Mark 9:24.
27   Psalm 118:32 (LXX).
28   Cf. John 15:12.
29   Ladder, Step 30:28.

11

✦━◈━✦━◈━✦━◈━✦━◈━✦

Service of the Akathist Hymn

April 3, 2020

SAINT GEORGE TROPEOFOROS GREEK ORTHODOX CHURCH
NEW YORK, NEW YORK

Beloved Brothers and Sisters in Christ,

Tonight we have gathered in the only Orthodox Church in Mid-Town Manhattan, the jewel-box we know as Saint George Tropeoforos, to chant on this Fifth Friday of Great Lent, the Akathist Hymn – this magnificent canticle in praise of our Παναγία, our merciful Mother and the Mother of our God.

Joining our voices with all the Churches across our Nation and around the world, we affirm that She is our Champion and Defender, as we intone:

Τῇ ὑπερμάχῳ στρατηγῷ τὰ νικητήρια,
ὡς λυτρωθεῖσα τῶν δεινῶν εὐχαριστήρια,
ἀναγράφω σοι ἡ πόλις σου, Θεοτόκε·
ἀλλ᾽ ὡς ἔχουσα τὸ κράτος ἀπροσμάχητον,

ἐκ παντοίων με κινδύνων ἐλευθέρωσον,
ἵνα κράζω σοί· Χαῖρε Νύμφη ἀνύμφευτε.

To You the Champion, we your City dedicate
a feast of victory and of thanksgiving,
as ones rescued out of sufferings, O Theotokos.
But as you are one with might that is invincible,
from all dangers that can be deliver us,
that we may cry to you:
Rejoice, Bride unwedded!

We cry out to the Mother of God, because we are Her City. Just as Constantinople was and still is in many ways the physical image of the Christian Γένος, all of us together constitute the City of God, which is not encompassed by any particular city of man, for as the Apostle Paul tells us in his Epistle to the Hebrews:

Οὐ γὰρ ἔχομεν ὧδε μένουσαν πόλιν, ἀλλὰ τὴν μέλλουσαν ἐπιζητοῦμεν.

For here we have no continuing city, but we seek one to come.[30]

This perspective on our life, that we have an eternal City which is to come, is not meant so that we ignore our present reality. Rather, it is to give us hope that whatever happens in this life, in this world, is not the final word in our existence. God has prepared for us both Σάββατον and Κυριακή, a Sabbath of rest from our labors here, and a Day of Resurrection unto Eternal Life. Such an affirmation makes our present life more vital and more precious.

Therefore, we can take heart, even in these most difficult days that no one ever expected to see in the modern era, the coming of a worldwide plague. But if all of us have been caught off guard, God has not. The Mother of God has not. And the Saints have not.

Our confidence is in God, and in the Church that abides in heavenly glory. It is our faith that binds us to the reality of Heaven, even when we cannot avail ourselves of the earthly temples within which we paint and sculpt and imitate the celestial Liturgy.

Just as these broadcasts via the internet strive to bring some of that experience into your homes, we know that God has already opened the doors of heaven into your hearts. And from above He rains down upon us blessings, and levels our anxieties and worries with His peace that passes all understanding.[31]

As the Prophet Isaiah foretold:

"Every valley shall be exalted, and every mountain and hill shall be made low; and the crooked shall be made straight, and the rough places plain."[32]

Therefore, my beloved people, allow God to fill and exalt the valleys of your doubt, to lower the mountains and hills of anxiety and worry that you face in this time of crisis, to straighten the crooked thoughts that distract you, and to smooth the rough places in your soul that stress and hurt you.

He will do all this and more if we will but allow it, through the prayers of our Champion, the Theotokos and Ever-Virgin Mary, and all the Saints.

Amen.

---

30   Hebrews 13:14.
31   Cf. Philippians 4:7.
32   Isaiah 40:4.

12

Fifth Sunday of Lent

April 5, 2020

SAINTS CONSTANTINE AND HELEN GREEK ORTHODOX CATHEDRAL
BROOKLYN, NEW YORK

Beloved Brothers and Sisters in Christ,

Today, on this Fifth Sunday of the Holy Fast, we broadcast from the Saints Constantine and Helen Cathedral in Brooklyn, New York, an historic parish that once served as the Cathedral of our Holy Archdiocese, and as such, is still honored with the name, "Cathedral."

Here we are at the end of Lent, and yet we are still in the middle of this unprecedented global pandemic, which continues to require that we employ the utmost caution even for only the clergy to perform the Divine Services. We all know at this point that the coming Holy Week and Pascha will be unlike anything we have ever experienced in our lives.

Just two days ago, I convened the Executive Committee of the Assembly of Bishops that includes all canonical Orthodox Hierarchs in the United States. Working with the brother Hierarchs, and after thorough consultation with public health and insurance officials, law enforcement, theologians, legal counsel, and pastoral care professionals, we had to come to the conclusion that this year the services of Holy Week and Pascha will have to remain as we are doing the services now, without the assembly of the Faithful. This is very painful for all of us, but the safety and health of our communities must be the most important consideration, as well as the directions of our civil authorities.

So as I celebrate here with Fr. Evagoras, the Deacons and the chanters, I ask myself, what is it that you, the Faithful, can receive from our continuing yet highly restricted worship? You are deprived of the Eucharist in our current conditions. How do you partake of the experience of God, even as we, the clergy, continue to offer the Liturgy for the health and salvation of the world?

It so happens that today we celebrate Saint Mary of Egypt, who spent forty years in the desert, deprived of receiving Holy Communion, and she waited patiently until the night she passed from this world to receive the Eucharist one last time. She is a great Saint – we give to her memory one of only fifty-two Sundays in the year – but she was "an angel in the flesh" and we are all not such angels.

Then I thought of the words of our Lord Jesus that He said to His Disciples, on the night He gave Himself for the life of the world:

Ἐν τῇ οἰκίᾳ τοῦ πατρός μου μοναὶ πολλαί εἰσιν....

In My Father's house are many mansions....[33]

With these encouraging words, the Lord Jesus Christ assured His Disciples and all of us of His presence at every time and in every place. In this hour of the global pandemic, which is isolating us from one another – a precaution for our health and the common good, I wanted to bring these words of our Lord and this message of comfort to you all, as a special exhortation not to despair, when a judicious confinement of our activities divides us from our communal worship and experience.

You see, the secret of the Christian life is that even when you are deprived of everything you recognize as your religion, the entirety of God is always within you. As the Lord said to His Disciples on the night in which He was betrayed, when all hope had disappeared:

Ἐάν τις ἀγαπᾷ με, τὸν λόγον μου τηρήσει, καὶ ὁ πατήρ μου ἀγαπήσει αὐτόν, καὶ πρὸς αὐτὸν ἐλευσόμεθα καὶ μονὴν παρ᾽ αὐτῷ ποιήσομεν.

If you love Me, you will keep My word, and My Father will love you, and We will come to you and make a cloister – a monastery – a μονή within you.[34]

This word, μονή, is the origin of the word "monastery" – the place where one dwells alone with God. The word only occurs twice in the New Testament, both in this wondrous soliloquy of our Lord Jesus Christ that is read as the first of the Twelve Gospels at the Thursday night Service of the Σταυρομένος.

It is our blessed assurance that God is always with us, and that we can always keep His word and be an entire monastery with the Holy Trinity residing in our hearts. Indeed, being that cloister of God – even in isolation from all others, is in fact the basis for our extension in and through the Spirit to every other person of faith.

My beloved Christians, be of good courage! We are never deprived of God! The only deprivation we can ever know is if we deprive ourselves of the experience of His abiding love, compassion, forgiveness and mercy. And we do this by depriving others of these very same virtues through selfishness and egocentrism.

During this time when we must, for the sake of our bodily health, refrain from community and even Holy Communion, let us reach down into our hearts for the sake of our souls. Let us enter inside one of those "many mansions" that our Lord Jesus Christ prepared for us. Deep within, we will find the communion that knows no physical form, but that endures forever, because God has truly come unto us – Μεθ᾽ ἡμῶν ὁ Θεός. Deep within, God is making each of our hearts into a monastery for Himself, mystically uniting us together in the one spiritual community of the Most Holy Trinity: Father, Son and Holy Spirit, Who is praised and glorified forever.

Amen.

---

33   John 14:2.
34   John 14:23.

13

Opening and Closing Remarks Nationwide Virtual Town Hall

"A Pastoral Word with Archbishop Elpidophoros of America"

April 11, 2020

ARCHDIOCESE HEADQUARTERS
NEW YORK, NEW YORK

My Beloved Brothers and Sisters in Christ,

First and foremost, I send to each and every one of you – whether you are with us through this webinar or otherwise – my heartfelt blessing and prayers for your health, and the health of your family and friends.

But I know as well that there are some among us who have lost loved ones to this pandemic, and I grieve with you. I want you to know that even in these most difficult circumstances, when we cannot even be present to bury our dearest, the prayer of the Church is strong and steady on their behalf and on yours. We pray for their eternal rest in God, and we pray for comfort in our time of mourning.

I also want to express my deepest appreciation and gratitude to all those on the front lines to aid in this critical time:

our healthcare personnel, doctors and nurses, and workers who are caring for the afflicted;

our firemen, police, emergency responders, and the civil officials who continue to make our society hold together for the sake of us all;

for all the people who staff our grocery stores, pharmacies and essential services, serving us every day at risk to themselves;

and for all our clergy who are continuing to serve the Faithful during this global pandemic, and who are prepared to serve Holy Week, the most difficult one in anyone's memory.

* * *

I am especially glad to be able to take questions and offer some perspectives today, but before I do, I wanted to share a few thoughts about this Holy Week before us.

When we began our Lenten journey, no one even suspected that we would arrive at such a point as this. We commenced our pilgrimage to Pascha in health, but we have arrived surrounded by sickness and death. What began for us as a normal season of spiritual intention, has ended in isolation from our churches and from one another.

In a way, we are somehow imitating our Lord Jesus Christ, Who arrived in Jerusalem to the shouts of "Hosanna," and then a few short days later heard that acclaim turn into "Crucify Him!" If you follow the liturgical texts of Holy Week, you see how the Lord begins with great cheering crowds, but then, little by little, the Disciples abandon Him to weariness, betrayal, arrest, denial, humiliation, torture, and ultimately death. As the Scripture prophesied: I will smite the Shepherd and the sheep will scatter.[35] The truth is when our Lord Jesus Christ died on the Cross, He died alone.

Therefore, my beloved Christians, know that in your most lonely and fearful moments – when your isolation is full of pain, worry, and fear – that our Lord Jesus Christ has already been there with you, He has been there for you, and He is with you now. Every day.

My prayer for all of you is that this Holy Week, when our lives and traditions have been so radically altered by this pandemic, you will find a new connection to your faith and to your Church, one that was unknown to you, or you did not think was possible.

Remember, the Church is the Body of the Lord, the Body of Christ. After the desolation of Holy Friday, and the Burial on Holy Saturday, Mary Magdalene thought that she had lost the Body of the Lord, but He appeared to her on the morning of the Resurrection.

He told her, "Touch Me not," but then called her to announce His Resurrection to His Disciples.[36]

Perhaps this Holy Week, when we must refrain from embraces and from the "*agape*" kiss, when we cannot touch our Faith and spiritual traditions as we have in the past, we might all respond to the call to announce the Resurrection to one another.

Let us use the means we have: video, telephone, even texting and social messaging, to tell each other and the whole world that Christ loves them, that He is risen from the dead, trampling down death by death, and that to all of us – here and in the beyond, He will grant eternal life.

51

And let us offer our love for each other and for the world with generous hearts, and forgive those who have hurt us. Our journey to Pascha was not so much interrupted as it was re-directed, to the interior person, to the center of the heart where God's love shines more brilliantly than the sun.

My beloved brothers and sisters in Christ, thank you for sharing this day with me, and by your intentions, sharing it with one another.

* * *

Closing Remarks

Thank you Demetria for moderating this webinar today, and thanks to all of you who participated. I am very grateful for you, because even though we are separated by distance – even the social distance that we need to preserve the health of ourselves, our families, and our neighbors – I feel your faith, I feel your hope, and I feel your love.

Today, you have reached out not just to me, but you have connected in some profound way to each other. Your silent presence on this call is an act of faith, and your questions remind us all that you are serious and believing Orthodox Christians, who love your Church and love each other.

I know that we will get through this together, and like the Israelites who passed through the Red Sea and escaped the Egypt full of plagues, we will come out on the other side of this pandemic.

Our world will be changed, but change is part of living in this world. The only eternal constant is God, Who is our hope, our refuge, and our salvation.

I wish all of you every spiritual blessing and continued good health this Holy Week and every week!

May you know in your hearts the power of His Resurrection, which extends through all eternity to every corner of creation.

Καλή Δύναμη, καὶ Καλή Ἀνάσταση σε ὅλους!

---

35 Zechariah 13:7.
36 Cf. John 20:17.

14

Saturday of Lazaros

April 11, 2020

ARCHANGEL MICHAEL GREEK ORTHODOX CHURCH
PORT WASHINGTON, NEW YORK

Beloved Brothers and Sisters in Christ,

Today, we are already on the road that is Holy Week, on our way to the Resurrection of Christ. It is a road with twists and turns, with great emotion, expectation, disappointment, sadness, and grievous loss. But it leads to glory!

So it is only fitting that we begin this odyssey with a resurrection, the great miracle of the raising from the dead of Lazaros by our Lord Jesus Christ.

We have returned to the Archangel Michael Church in Port Washington, New York for a very special reason. Here, for many years now, the Divine Liturgy on the Saturday of Lazaros has been specifically celebrated for persons with special needs. And even though we must continue to observe the Divine Services in a precautionary and restricted way, I wanted very much to hold fast to this tradition.

We must remember those who need special care and attention, because they are often considered to be weak, by those who forget that God has chosen the weak.[37]

And they are too often unseen and unheard. They need and deserve our advocacy. They need our consideration. They need our love.

They need us to be of help to them, especially in this time of the pandemic. They need us to help them live free and unhindered lives, to have the kind of lives we want for ourselves.

So that is why I traveled here with my *synodia* to Port Washington this morning, to this wonderful Archangel Michael Church, where the ministry to those with special needs began in the Direct Archdiocese District. And since then, many parishes have followed with similar ministries of their own.

But today, the Saturday of Lazaros, seems to be the most fitting time, because it inaugurates Holy Week, our most sacred week of the year, and because there is a specific commandment of the Lord that commends all of us to this ministry.

When Lazaros was raised from the dead, he was not as the Lord Who, not many days hence, will raise Himself by the power of God. Here is the key difference as told in today's Gospel:

And Lazaros, who to that very moment was dead, emerged with his hands and feet bound together by the charnel linens. His face also had been tightly wrapped and was covered by the face-shroud.[38]

Unlike in the Resurrection of our Lord, whose grave clothes were set to one side, and whose face covering, the *soudarion*, was folded apart from the rest.[39]

Lazaros, now alive after four days in the tomb, is still bound with the winding bandages. He needs help. He needs to be loosened. He needs to be set free.

Therefore, when the Lord sees him come forth in this state from the tomb, He commands the bystanders with these words: "Loose him and let him go forth!"[40]

My beloved friends, this commandment is meant for us. The Lord calls us to unbind those whose lives are impeded by barriers not of their own making.

He commands us to step up and provide a way of emancipation for those who need that extra effort.

He calls us to loose those who are fettered, either in body or mind, and who want to walk in the light of the Lord. But they are restricted by the mortal bonds of this world, just as Lazaros was tightly wrapped in the winding bandages. Lazaros could not free himself and walk to Christ, Who was his dearest friend. Others had to step up and help.

Should we not also grant a degree of freedom to our brothers and sisters who are bound, sometimes far away from our parishes, and need our help to come to partake of the Liturgy, to walk to Christ?

Right now – in this moment when we must observe legal and health restrictions in this crisis, we are all homebound, separated from the Liturgy of the Church. Now we have a tangible experience of what our special needs Faithful know every Sunday of the year.

It is my fervent prayer that when we are able to return to a regular Church life, we will not forget those with special needs in our own community and in our general public. Like Lazaros, they often do not speak on their own behalf.

But they are as worthy of our love and attention as the dearest members of our own families. Because we are one family, the family of God.

I pray fervently that this Holy Week will be a blessing to you, and you will be a blessing to others. May you open your hearts to the Divine Presence which is "everywhere present and fills all things."

And may you find space in your hearts for the special needs of our special brothers and sisters. You will discover that through your acts of kindness and love, the miracle of the Resurrection will become your very own, in deed and in truth.

Καλή Δύναμη, καὶ Καλή Ἀνάσταση!

---

37   Cf. I Corinthians 1:27.
38   John 11:44.
39   Cf. John 20:6,7.
40   John 11:44.

15

Palm Sunday

April 12, 2020

Holy Trinity Archdiocesan Cathedral
New York, New York

Beloved Brothers and Sisters in Christ,

*Σήμερον ἡ χάρις τοῦ ἁγίου Πνεύματος, ἡμᾶς συνήγαγε, καὶ πάντες
αἴροντες τὸν Σταυρόν σου λέγομεν· Εὐλογημένος ὁ ἐρχόμενος, ἐν
ὀνόματι Κυρίου· Ὡσαννὰ ἐν τοῖς ὑψίστοις.*

*Today the grace of the Holy Spirit has gathered us together, and as
we all take up Your Cross we cry out: Blessed is He Who comes in
the Name of the Lord! Hosanna in the highest!*

Indeed, my beloved Christians, it is the grace of the Holy Spirit
that brings us together today – whether by video or audio, or most
simply and indeed most purely, by the intentions of our hearts – it is
the Spirit of God Who unites us on this blessed Palm Sunday.

Today, our Western Christian Brothers and Sisters are celebrating
Easter – and we wish them every joy.

But we are not there yet. Although we already commenced yesterday, as today's Gospel says, "six days before the Passover,"[42] in the aftermath of the greatest of our Lord's miracles, the raising of Lazaros. This σημεῖον, this sign, is the statement of our Lord Jesus Christ to the world of His love for us, and it is the backdrop of our present Feast.

The commotion stirred up in Jerusalem and in Judea, from Bethany where the miracle occurred, to the Temple precincts into which Jesus marched on this Sunday of the Palms, all of this signaled something extraordinary to the people. They hailed Jesus as their King, remembering the prophecy of Zechariah:

> Rejoice greatly, O daughter of Zion! Shout, O daughter of Jerusalem! Behold, your King is coming to you; He is just and having salvation, humble and riding on a donkey, a colt, the foal of a donkey.[43]

When they saw Christ on the foal of the donkey, they remembered this prophecy, and they believed that Jesus was a king who had come to free them from the Roman oppressors. They did not understand that His "Kingdom is not of this world."[44]

They did not realize that this Nazarene from Galilee was, in truth, born in Bethlehem of Judea. He was no Galilean by blood at all, but rather a direct descendent from Judah, the fourth son of Jacob. Thus, they did not connect him with the *other* prophecy:

> Binding his foal unto the vine, and his donkey's colt unto the choice vine; He washed his garments in wine, and His clothes in the blood of grapes.[45]

You see, my friends, our Lord is the True Vine, and by riding upon the donkey colt – an animal considered unclean in Judaism and thus symbolizing all Gentiles – He binds our fate and that of every human being to His own. He takes upon Himself the salvation of all the Gentiles as well as all the Jewish People, not just the one man, Lazaros, whom He raised from the dead.

And what are the garments that He will wash in "wine … in the blood of grapes?" They are the human nature of every person who has ever lived or will ever live. He comes to cleanse us, to purify our hearts and our humanity, and in order to do so, He has to shed His Precious Blood. He marches into Jerusalem on this Palm Sunday to unleash a river of love, a torrent of mercy, and a flood of forgiveness.

The crowds see only their faint hope of an earthly King:

a King without an army,

a King on a humble donkey – not a magnificent steed,

a King without a crown.

They cast their garments before Him. The cut down branches of palms and cover the road with them. They offer what they can, even in their ignorance of the moment. They see only an earthly solution to their worldly problems. But again, the Kingdom of the Lord Jesus Christ is not of this world. And in only five days they will go from cheering for their 'King' to crying, "Crucify Him!"[47]

Therefore, we must decide for ourselves. How will we meet the King of Glory? The One Who is coming this Holy Week to shed His Precious Blood for us and to wash our human nature clean.

Today, we may not be able to gather with our palms, but we can still lay down our garments before Him. We can have the intention to offer to the Lord the fullness of our human nature.

Each and every one of us – in our own way, can pave His rocky road to Golgotha with our love for one another, with our compassion for those who are suffering, and with our forgiveness for those who have wronged us. This is why the hymn I began with exhorts us to willingly 'take up His Cross' like Simon of Cyrene, although he was forced to by the Roman soldiers.[48]

By loving those we think unworthy of our love, by our empathy for those whom we do not know, and especially by forgiving those who have wronged us, we share in the Cross of the Lord. We share in His Holy Passion, τά Ἅγια Πάθη Του, by which His Holy Body is broken and His Precious Blood is shed for the life of the world.

And when the day comes, and we can receive Holy Communion together again as the Assembly of the Church, you will know more profoundly what it is to be a Christian.

You will know with assurance that you are the ones who bear His Name, not only outwardly for the world to see, but inwardly where the truth of the Faith will drum in your heart with every beat.

You will know what it is to suffer for redemption, not for the randomness, as we know in this pandemic.

You will know that the Cross is the key that unlocks the gates of Paradise, and not an ancient instrument of death.

And you will know the same deep knowledge that Lazaros knew, when he was called forth from his grave after four days. That God is the Source and Wellspring of life, and by His own Glorious Resurrection, He grants eternal life to us all.

May this Holy Week – this extraordinary Holy Week – be the most blessed of your life.

Καλή Δύναμη, καὶ Καλή Ἀνάσταση!

41   Prokeimenon of Palm Sunday Matins.
42   John 12:1
43   Zechariah 9.9.
44   John 18:36.
45   Genesis 49:11.
46   John15:1.
47   John 19:15.
48   Cf. Matthew 27:32.

16

First Bridegroom Service

Great and Holy Monday - April 12, 2020

ARCHDIOCESE CHAPEL OF SAINT PAUL
NEW YORK, NEW YORK

Φθάσαντες πιστοί, τὸ σωτήριον Πάθος Χριστοῦ τοῦ Θεοῦ!

W e have arrived, O Faithful, at the saving Passion of Christ our God!

We have indeed arrived, my beloved Brothers and Sisters in Christ, at this first of the Holy Week services that we are sharing with you from your Archdiocese Chapel of Saint Paul in New York City.

As you know, we serve this Matins of Holy Monday in conditions as confining, or even more confining, than the Catacombs were for our early Christian forebears.

At this beginning of Holy Week, we must be as the Disciples after the Resurrection – behind shut doors, *τῶν θυρῶν κεκλεισμένων*.[49] But unlike the Disciples of that moment – before they knew of the Resurrection, we do not cower in fear. We gather in love. We gather in faith! We gather in hope! For we know the end of the story!

My beloved Christians, how fortunate we are indeed. We know that after the pain, comes the gladness. After the suffering, comes the glory. And after the darkness, comes the dawn.

Therefore, as we embrace the Bridegroom Who presents Himself to us, Who comes to us in the middle of the night, ἐν τῷ μέσῳ τῆς νυκτός, we embrace Him as He is.

He is the *Philanthopos* – the One Who loves humankind. The One for Whom no sacrifice is too great, no distance too far, no humiliation too extreme.

The Lord offered everything – His Humanity and His Divinity, subjecting Himself to suffering and death.

He traveled the greatest span that could ever be bridged – the Uncreated to the Created, from Heaven to Earth.

And as the Apostle Paul says:

He emptied himself, taking the form of a slave, born in the likeness of humankind. Being found in human configuration,
He humbled himself, became obedient unto death, even death of the Cross.[50]

His humiliation was total and complete, and it is manifest in the Icon of the Bridegroom that we bring forth and venerate today.

Indeed, my beloved Sisters and Brothers, what bridegroom was ever adorned like this?

Instead of shining garments, a robe of mockery.

Instead of a garland of flowers, a crown of thorns.

Instead of a scepter of dignity, a reed of humiliation.

Instead of hands reaching out to His beloved, they are fettered in captivity.

This is our Bridegroom, the One Who comes to us – the Church – His most beloved and precious Bride. And as Isaiah so rightly prophesied:

He has no form nor comeliness; and when we see Him, there is no beauty that we should desire Him. He was despised and rejected of men; a Man of Sorrows, and acquainted with grief: and we hid our faces from Him; He was despised, and we esteemed Him not.[51]

Therefore, we must look beyond the outward appearance, to His heart that burns with love for every single human being.

And we will see His robe of mockery as a covering for our sins.

His crown of thorns as our adoption into the royal family of God.

His reed of humiliation as the battering ram that bursts asunder the gates of hell.

And His chained hands as our emancipation from death.

Our Bridegroom spares nothing in His pursuit of our love. He will never accept how we spurn His affection out of our sin, our ignorance, our guilt, and our shame.

He has come this Holy Week to liberate us, and to take us into His Bridal Chamber, the sacred Θάλαμος where we will begin to understand our purpose as human beings.

To love as He loved us, to forgive as He forgave us, and to show mercy in every aspect of our lives, just as He pours His mercy and compassion upon us ἐν παντὶ καιρῷ καὶ πάσῃ ὥρᾳ.

My beloved Christians, this Holy Week – a week unlike any other – let us welcome the Bridegroom of our souls into our innermost selves. Let us embrace His love for us, just as a happy and joyful bride awaits the embrace of her bridegroom.

And let us prepare our hearts, minds, and souls to experience the Resurrection of Christ in ways that we never anticipated, but that our Lord will accomplish, through His grace and love for all humankind. Amen.

---

49   John 20:19.
50   Philippians 2:7,8.
51   Isaiah 53:2,3.

17

Second Bridegroom Service

Great and Holy Tuesday - April 13, 2020

Archdiocese Chapel of Saint Paul
New York, New York

My beloved Brothers and Sisters in Christ,

Just two days ago, I had the wonderful opportunity to speak to thousands of faithful who participated in the nationwide webinar on the Saturday of Lazaros. In the course of the hour, someone asked me if I thought that this pandemic was a sign of the End of Days, a signal that the Second Coming of the Lord was near. I replied that this is unknown, even as the Lord Himself said:

> *But of that day and hour no one knows, not even the angels of Heaven, but My Father only.*[52]

I also reminded everyone that it is not just about when the Lord will return as He promised; it is about when we shall go forth to meet Him at the end of *our* days.

Just as there is no guarantee to anyone that they will live in the Last Days, there is most certainly a definite guarantee that our days on this earth are numbered. This pandemic is a painful reminder of our fragility and our mortality. And there is a seed of wisdom in this knowledge, one that germinates in the Parable of the Ten Virgins.

That is the reason for placing this Parable in tonight's *Nymphios* Service. The Five wise, and the Five foolish. Their journey to meet the Bridegroom is an image of the journey of every soul. Some are prepared to meet the Lord, and some are not. But it is inevitable that He will come.

Listen to the words of our Lord Jesus Christ:

> *Then will the Kingdom of Heaven be likened to ten virgins, who took their lamps and went out to meet the Bridegroom. Now, five of the virgins were wise, and five were foolish. When the foolish each picked up their lamps, they did not take any oil along. But the wise took jars of oil along with their lamps.*[53]

Each group of Five starts out with a lamp that is lit and full. This symbolizes every human being because we all have the same capacity for God. Each of us, even before our Baptism, is made in the image of God. We are beings that are created for communion and for community. Just as the Holy Trinity is One, and yet Three. We are made for relationships that spring from love, just as the Holy Trinity is the fountainhead of love; for God is love, ὁ Θεός ἀγάπη ἐστίν.[54]

But for most of us, life is not lived in a single day or a single year. It is a journey, and we need to replenish the oil that feeds the flame of our love throughout our lives. For some, this means marriage and family. For others, it means a life of chaste service – often in the Church, and also in the world. But however we live our lives, if we are wise, if we are intuitive, if we are prudent and thoughtful, we will cultivate a life that is loving and altruistic. That is what it means for the Five Wise Virgins to be carrying the jars of oil.

The Five Foolish ones are examples of lives that began with a capacity for love, but through a self-centered, selfish existence, they exhausted their God-given human grace.

But then – *in the middle of the night, there was a shout, 'Behold the Bridegroom comes!'*[55] This is not the Second Coming of our Lord, as much as it is the moment when life is at an end and we come to Him. In that moment, the Five Foolish ask the Five Wise for some oil. But you cannot seize the virtue or the merit of others. You must live your own life, and be judged by your own deeds. Even if you run to do good at the very end, you may not have enough time, as the Parable says:

> *But as the five foolish virgins went off to buy the oil, the Bridegroom arrived. And the five who were prepared went in with Him to the marriage feast, and the door was shut.*[56]

This is why we watch. This is why we remain vigilant in our spiritual lives. This is why we are diligent and not lazy in pursuing righteousness, and truth, and always love.

My beloved Christians, remember the saying of the Lord:

> *But of that day and hour no one knows, not even the angels of Heaven, but My Father only.*[57]

This could be said of the end of each and every one of us, not just the Second and Glorious Coming of the Lord.

That is why in this intense week, this Holy Week, we take stock of our lives, and we examine our deeds, to see how we are really living. Are we like the Wise? Or are we like the Foolish. Do we refresh our hearts with love for even the unlovable? Or do we waste the precious moments of our life in only selfish endeavors?

Therefore, we cry out:

Ἀλλ' ὦ Νυμφίε Χριστέ, μετὰ τῶν φρονίμων ἡμᾶς συναρίθμησον Παρθένων, καὶ τῇ ἐκλεκτῇ σου σύνταξον ποίμνῃ, καὶ ἐλέησον ἡμᾶς.

O Christ our Bridegroom, unite us with the wise virgins and join us to Your chosen flock, and have mercy on us and save us.[58]

Amen.

---

52 Matthew 24:36.
53 Matthew 25:1-4.
54 I John 4:8.
55 Matthew 25:6.
56 Matthew 25:10.
57 Matthew 24:36.
58 Verse of the Synaxarion of Matins of Holy and Great Tuesday.

18

Third Bridegroom Service

Great and Holy Wednesday - April 14, 2020

ARCHDIOCESE CHAPEL OF SAINT PAUL
NEW YORK, NEW YORK

Dear Brothers and Sisters in Christ,

We have arrived at our final Nymphios Service for Holy Week, one that is beloved by all Orthodox Christians for the famous hymn of Kassiani that concludes this Matins of Holy Wednesday.

This magnificent hymn begins:

Κύριε, ἡ ἐν πολλαῖς ἁμαρτίαις περιπεσοῦσα γυνή...

O Lord, the woman who had fallen into many sins ...

It tells the story of an anointing of the Lord that happens before His Passion in the house of Simon the Leper, and in many ways mirrors the other anointing of the Lord in Bethany, by Mary the sister of Lazaros.

In both instances, the women served as preemptive Myrrh-Bearers, whose acts of love and devotion performed a great service for the

Lord in advance. One was nameless, a known sinner, and a stranger to the Lord. The other was Mary, a dear friend, and disciple who sat at His feet to hear "the one thing needful."[59] But they both chose to offer their most precious possession, in a mystical foreshadowing of the Resurrection.

You might ask, how does this anointing foretell the Rising from the dead of our Lord? If you recall the aftermath of the Crucifixion, the righteous Women, led by the Holy Theotokos and Mary Magdalene – and aided by Joseph of Arimathea and Nikodemos – hastened to bury the Sacred Body of our Lord before sundown, the beginning of the Sabbath.

But the sky was dark, because the "Sun of Righteousness"[60] had eclipsed in His willing death on the Cross.[61] The Day of Preparation, which is why Friday is called Παρασκευή in Greek, was almost over. And this meant there was no time to finish the proper anointing in accordance with Jewish custom.

It is the reason why the Women returned to the Tomb early on Sunday morning, very early – λίαν πρωΐ, as the Gospel of the Resurrection says, διαγενομένου τοῦ σαββάτου, "when the Sabbath had passed." They came back to anoint Christ, Who is already the Anointed One, which is the very meaning of the word, Χριστός.

But they had already been anticipated by the Sinful Woman, and by Mary the sister of Lazaros.

As we chant in the Hymn of Kassiani, where it says of the Woman who had fallen into many sins,

τὴν σὴν αἰσθομένη Θεότητα, μυροφόρου ἀναλαβοῦσα τάξιν…

sensing Your Divinity, she took upon herself the rank of a Myrrh-Bearer…

She sensed the Divinity of the Lord in spite of her sinfulness. She approached the Lord, humbly, standing behind Him like a servant. She wept upon His feet and dried them with her hair. And then, taking an alabaster jar of very costly myrrh, she broke the jar, and anointed the feet of the Lord.[63]

This act of offering is majestic in so many ways.

She did not join the table of the host, but acted only as a servant.

She poured forth her confession silently through her weeping, and by kissing the feet of Christ.

She dried our Lord's feet, moistened by her tears, with her hair, which, for a Jewish woman, was her most precious adornment.

And finally, she took a jar of the most precious myrrh, and opened it the only way it could be opened, by breaking it, for such vials were always sealed for just one use. Her offering was so great, so costly, that the Disciples were offended and asked the Lord: "εἰς τί ἡ ἀπώλεια αὔτη – why this waste?"[64] They even justified their outrage by invoking the cause of the poor.

But the women remained silent, never uttering a word of defense for her actions. She left her defense to Christ and to Christ alone. What an example she is to every one of us!

Thus, while the Disciples berated her for her act of generosity, the Lord rewarded her and commended her "good deed."[65]

While His host, Simon the Leper, judged our Lord for allowing the sinful Woman to touch Him, the Lord taught Simon a lesson in mercy, and sent the woman away pardoned, healed, saved, and in peace.[66]

While Peter, on the Night of the Mystical Supper, would protest the Lord washing his feet, the Woman who had fallen into many sins washed the feet of our Master Christ with her tears.

While Judas would give our Lord a kiss of betrayal in the Garden of Gethsemane, the sinful Woman kissed "the feet whose sound Eve heard at dusk in Paradise" – of which Kassiani sings.

While the Roman soldiers tossed lots for His garments as the Lord hung naked on the Cross, the Woman dried and covered His feet with hair.

And finally, while the Righteous Women came to the Tomb to anoint Him and finish their custom, and they found Him not! The Woman finished their work before they even began. She anointed Him with more than precious ointment, she anointed Him with total and unconditional love.

My beloved Christians, the sinful Woman acted before the Passion. And we are here now in this Holy Week, two thousand years after the Passion, but we can still act. We can still offer.

This week is happening for us as if we were truly there, whether we can physically attend the services or not. Because this and every Holy Week happens in the liturgical time that is called συμβεβηκότος καιρός – time that compresses past, present and even the future into one stream of reality, with all the attendant attributes and consequences.

Therefore, we are, this evening, in the house of Simon the Leper. We are standing in the same room, but it is up to us to choose whom we shall be.

The one who judges the deeds of others?

The one who complains about the waste, the cost, the value of another's gift?

Or the one who offers true and sincere repentance,

who rains down tears upon the feet of the Lord's Body,

who offers the most precious gift of heart and soul,

and who perceives the Resurrection before there is any manifestation.

May we join with that Sinful Woman in all her excellencies, in all her faith, in all perceptions, and thus announce beforehand the Resurrection of our Lord and Savior Jesus Christ, who is blessed forever. Amen.

---

59 Luke 10:42.
60 Malachi 4:2.
61 Cf. Luke 23:45a (Greek: τοῦ ἡλίου ἐκλείποντος…)
62 Cf. Mark 16:1,2.
63 Cf. Luke 19:37,38.
64 Matthew 26:8.
65 Cf. Matthew 26:10.
66 Cf. Luke 7:39-50.

19

Service of Holy Unction

Great and Holy Wednesday - April 14, 2020

ARCHDIOCESE CHAPEL OF SAINT PAUL
NEW YORK, NEW YORK

Beloved Brothers and Sisters in the Lord,

We have come to this midpoint in Holy Week, where traditionally the Church offers the Sacrament of Holy Unction to the faithful, for healing of body and soul, and for the forgiveness of sins.[67] This year, our petitions for healing are all the more urgent, as we continue to face the challenge of this global pandemic.

Although we attempted to find a way to convey the Sacrament of Unction to you, it was decided by all the Orthodox Bishops in America that this would not be wise, especially now when the virus is peaking in many parts of the country. But I want to say something to you tonight that may surprise you, that may challenge your understanding of this Sacrament of healing.

Yes, the Mystery of Anointing with Holy Oil goes back to the days of the Apostles, and we know that tangible objects that have been sanctified by prayer and by the Holy Spirit are designed to be

79

shared in the community. These objects are what we might call, "the hem of His garment" that the sick woman yearned to touch so that she would be made whole.[68] They are the material substances that transmit a spiritual reality for health of body and soul. But we should remember that this woman, who had lived with a physical affliction for twelve years:

an affliction that was considered unclean in Judaism,

and an affliction on which she had spent her entire fortune to no avail,

we should remember that she had the intention and purpose before she touched that hem of His garment.

She was like, but perhaps not equal to, the Roman Centurion of Capernaum.[69] The Centurion asked the Lord to heal his servant, and when Christ agreed to come to his home to fulfill his request, the Centurion said this:

Lord, I am not worthy that You should come under my roof: but speak the word only, and my servant shall be healed.[70]

The Centurion understood authority from his military experience and from being in command. From his faith alone, he perceived an analogous spiritual authority in our Lord Jesus Christ. Thus he did not need to see the physical manifestation of the spiritual reality. He knew that the healing would take place on the word of the Lord alone, and the Lord marveled at his faith.

My beloved Christians, we also know this can be so, because as the Apostle Paul says:

πίστις ἐλπιζομένων ὑπόστασις, πραγμάτων ἔλεγχος οὐ βλεπομένων,

faith is the substance of things hoped for, the evidence of things unseen.[71]

Therefore, even in these constrained and restricted circumstances, we are able to invoke the Holy Spirit from anywhere. The oil may be here in this one location, but the Spirit of God is "everywhere present and filling all things," – πανατχοῦ παρὼν καὶ τὰ πάντα πληρῶν.

The true vessel of the Spirit is the Lord Himself. He was revealed as the most precious container of the Heavenly Myrrh when the Holy Spirit descended upon Him in the form of a dove on the Day of His Baptism.

And just yesterday, in the story of the Anointing of Christ by the sinful Woman, the image of her alabaster jar of precious myrrh reflects the truth of our Lord. He broke Himself open upon the Cross through His Holy Passion and Death in order to unleash in the world the gift of the Spirit.

Remember how He says in the Mystical Supper: "This is my Body, which is *broken* for you?"[72] And yet the Scripture maintains that "not a bone of him was broken,"[73] even giving the details of exactly what happened after the Lord had expired on the Cross:

Because it was the Day of Preparation, the religious authorities asked Pilate to have their legs broken and their bodies removed, so that they might not remain on the cross during the Sabbath, because that particular Sabbath day was especially important. So the soldiers went and broke the legs of the first man, and those of the other man who was crucified with Jesus. But when they came to Jesus and saw that he was already dead, they did not break his legs.[74]

So, my beloved Christians? I ask you: What part of the Lord was broken? It was the Heart. It was His loving, compassionate, merciful heart. His heart that loves us so very much, that there was no length to which He would not go to save us.

And His Precious Body, broken open in the Eucharist, broken open upon the Cross, is like that precious jar of myrrh, which "filled the house with the fragrance of the myrrh."[75]

The house that our Lord has filled with the sweet savor of His sacrificial love is the entire universe. And tonight, you are able to obtain that grace, that spiritual sweetness, that healing touch right where you are, in your homes.

Open your heart like the Women who broke open their vials of precious ointment. Allow yourself to break down the barriers that block your mind, your emotions, your spirit and your soul from the encounter with the Living God.

The Unction we offer this evening is present with you even now through the Spirit of God. Until you can touch this "hem of His garment," allow yourself to receive healing grace as did the Centurion.

Thus, you will find healing of body and soul, and forgiveness for all your sins in the glorious Resurrection of our Lord, God, and Savior, Jesus Christ.

Amen.

---

67   Cf. Iakovos (James) 5:14,15.
68   Cf. Matthew 9:20-22.
69   Cf. Matthew 8:5-10.
70   Matthew 8:8.
71   Hebrews 111.
72   I Corinthians 11:24.
73   John 19:36; Exodus 12:46; Psalm 34:20 (33:20 LXX).
74   John 19:31-33.
75   John 12:3.

20

Vesperal Divine Liturgy
of Holy and Great Thursday
April 16, 2020

Archdiocese Chapel of Saint Paul
New York, New York

Beloved Brothers and Sisters in the Lord,

Today – in the midst of this crisis that separates you from the Divine Liturgies throughout the Nation and the world – we celebrate the Institution of this very same Liturgy.

The Upper Room, the Ἀνώγαιον as it called in Greek,[76] where our Lord gathered His Disciples for the Mystical Supper, could really be called the first Christian Ναός, the first church building. And the preparations for the Passover that the Lord instructed the Disciples to make,[77] were more a symbolic setting for the radical and transformative Meal that He prepared, in order to establish His Kingdom upon earth, as it is in Heaven.[78]

In this first Divine Liturgy, the Lord transfigured the Feast of Passover, the commemoration of the liberation of the Jewish People from Egypt through the death of the Egyptian first-born. The freedom of the Jewish Passover extended only to this world, not to the world to come.

In its place, our Lord Jesus Christ became Himself the Passover, Who is sacrificed for the life of the world. As the Apostle Paul says:

> *For truly, Christ our Pascha has been sacrificed for us. Therefore, let us keep the Feast – not with old leaven, nor with the leaven of wickedness and evil, but with the unleavened bread of sincerity and truth.*[79]

In this Sacred Meal He shared with His Disciples, the Lord Jesus Christ completely reversed the use of Leavened and Unleavened, ἄρτος and ἄζυμος. The former becomes the bread of the Eucharist, leaving behind the unleavened bread of the Passover. The latter become the symbol of the sincerity and truth with which we must approach the Eucharist, even as the image of the "leaven of wickedness and evil" is a symbol for a heart unprepared to receive Holy Communion.

My beloved Christians, many of you during this time have had many questions about the Eucharist and the pandemic. You have asked, "Can we become sick from Holy Communion?" "Will the λαβίδα, the Holy Spoon, make us ill?"

But what does the Scripture teach? Listen to what Saint Paul says about receiving the Body and Blood when we are unworthy, when the leaven of our souls is full of "wickedness and evil."

> *Therefore, whoever eats This Bread or drinks of the Cup of the Lord unworthily will be guilty of the Body and Blood of the Lord. Let each person do a rigorous self-examination, and then – in this way, eat of the Bread and drink of the Cup. For if you eat and drink unworthily, you eat and drink to the condemnation of your own*

selves, because you do not discern the Body of the Lord. This is the reason why many among you have become sick, as well as a number of you have died.[80]

At first, this seems shocking to us, but you must listen carefully to what he is saying. Saint Paul does not say that the Body and Blood of the Lord can make anyone sick, much less cause their death. The Body and Blood of the Lord are for our health and salvation.

What Saint Paul does say is *how* we receive Holy Communion makes a difference. And this is not a matter of custom or belief; it is a matter of understanding and spiritual practice.

Do we discern the Body of the Lord? Discerning the "Body of the Lord" is much more about recognizing your interdependence and interconnectedness with your fellow members of the Body, your brothers and sisters in Christ. It is not just about believing that the Bread and Wine are indeed the Flesh and Blood of the Lord, which is an immutable truth, declared by the Lord Himself.[81]

The questions we should be asking are: How do we esteem others? How do we value them? Are we critical and judgmental of others, and their motivations, intentions, and actions?

Consider these words of the Lord:

Μὴ κρίνετε, ἵνα μὴ κριθῆτε.

Judge not that you not be judged.[82]

Or Saint Paul again:

Σὺ τίς εἶ ὁ κρίνων ἀλλότριον οἰκέτην;

Who are you to judge someone else's servant?[83]

We must be attentive not only to how we, as individuals, accept the beliefs of the Church. We must look deeply into the Mystery of the Faith, and behold the Body of Christ which is His Church, and embrace all its members with love, compassion, mercy, and forgiveness.

This is the meaning of the true passing over from a mortal life to an immortal life. This is the liberation that comes only from the Firstborn of the dead – τόν Πρωτότοκον ἐκ τῶν νεκρῶν, as Saint Paul says.[84] The Firstborn of the dead saves not only the firstborn who were cursed, but all the children of humankind.

Thus, we see that in every way, Pascha surpasses the Passover. And the Lamb of God liberates humanity from the barbarism of animal sacrifice and the spilling of blood.

But the Blood of the Lord is shed for our sakes, not as a substitution for our punishment. Saint Gregory the Theologian, Archbishop of Constantinople says that His blood was shed on the Cross:

on account of the Incarnation, and because Humanity must be sanctified by the Humanity of God, that He might deliver us Himself, overcome the tyrant, and draw us to Himself.[85]

My beloved Christians, we receive the Body that was broken for us, and the Blood that was shed for us, in order to remake our shared humanity by the Divine Humanity of our Lord Jesus Christ. He is our Pascha, the Lamb of God Who takes away the sin of the world.[86] Who takes away our sins. And the sins of all our brothers and sisters. In them we behold the Body of Christ, the One, Holy, Catholic, and Apostolic Church we confess every time we recite the Creed.

Every Divine Liturgy partakes of the Mystical Supper, whereby we receive the re-creation of our being by the Humanity of God.

May God grant that we always receive Holy Communion worthily, discerning His Body, and seeing the face of His Beloved Son in the face of every person, receiving the least as we receive the greatest – with humility, respect, forgiveness, and love. Amen.

---

76   Luke 22:12.
77   Cf. Luke 22:7-13.
78   Cf. Luke 22:18, and the Lord's Prayer (Matthew 6:9-13).
79   I Corinthians 5:7b,8.
80   I Corinthians 11:27-30.
81   Cf. John 6:55.
82   Matthew 7:1.
83   Romans 14:4.
84   Colossians 1:18.
85   Oration 45, On the Holy Pascha, XXII.
86   Cf. John 1:29.

21

Service of the Twelve Gospels

Matins of Great and Holy Friday - April 16, 2020

ARCHDIOCESE CHAPEL OF SAINT PAUL
NEW YORK, NEW YORK

Dear Brothers and Sisters in Christ,

Perhaps there is no other service of Great and Holy Week that brings us into the presence of God's love more than this Matins of Holy Friday. Tonight we read the Twelve Gospel περικοπές that take us from the Soliloquy of Love to the Burial of our Lord in the Tomb of the Rich Man from Arimathea.

Every year, these Twelve Gospels bring us the most important words ever spoken by our Lord, and they also bring us the agonizing details of His Arrest, Trial, Torture, Crucifixion, Death and Burial.

In these Gospels, we hear what are commonly referred to as the "Seven Last Words" of the Lord. These seven utterances, the last words that He spoke in his earthly existence from His Cross, each one is a sermon of the greatest significance and meaning.

Although you have heard all of these "Seven Words" in the course of this evening's service – I would share one of them yet again with you, my beloved Faithful. I would share the one that I believe speaks to us most profoundly in this present global crisis.

In His agony upon the Cross, in His pain and unspeakable suffering, our Lord Jesus Christ cried out:

Ἐλωΐ Ἐλωΐ, λιμᾶ σαβαχθανί;

This is not Greek, but Aramaic, his native tongue for:

O My God, My God, why have You abandoned Me?[87]

He exclaims this agonizing cry – whose origin is in the Psalms of David:

Ὁ Θεός, ὁ Θεός μου, πρόσχες μοι· ἵνα τί ἐγκατάλιπές με;[88]

And we are left to wonder. Does He cry out in anger? In horror? In fear? In utter abandonment?

And we ask ourselves: How could God abandon His Only-Begotten Son?

Or: How could Christ feel any separation from his Father, with Whom He shared Pre-Eternal Glory before the created world came to exist?

And if these questions have challenged theologians and philosophers through the ages, how much more so do they challenge us, who live in these difficult days of a worldwide and virulent pandemic.

Therefore, my beloved Christians, I am asking that you consider the words of our Lord not as a mere personal cry of agony, but as an invocation, an entreaty, an appeal on behalf of us all.

You see, our Lord Jesus Christ was much more than a human being, He was the God-Man Who was fully Divine and fully Human, as the definition of the Ecumenical Council says:

ἀσυγχύτως, ἀτρέπτως, ἀδιαιρέτως, ἀχωρίστως.

unconfusedly, unchangeably, indivisibly, inseparably[90]

Total God and Total Human. And in that humanity of His own Divine Person, He enfolded every human being who had ever lived before Him, was living during His earthly ministry, or would ever live thereafter.

He took upon Himself not only our sins and sinfulness, but our fears, our anxieties, our worries, our insecurities and all our pain – whether of the body, mind, or soul. All of this weight – this unfathomable burden – He took to the Cross.

In His Humanity, He began by living a perfect life without ever sinning. Then He incorporated all of us into Himself at the Mystical Supper, where as the Holy Chrysostom says, He drank His own Blood.[91] And before the Lord was seized in the Garden of Gethsemane, we see Him in the agony of His prayer, beseeching His Father to let "this cup" – the cup of suffering, pain and death – "pass from Me."[92]

He understands our fear of death, because He felt it – every human beings' fear of dying – and He felt it in one moment of time. Is it any wonder then, that in Gethsemane – which means "olive press" – that the Lord sweat blood? The Gospel record is clear and even graphic:

As He prayed more intensely, He was wracked with agony. His sweat rained down on the ground like bloody clots.[93]

Finally, upon the Cross, in these excruciating words, He expressed the ultimate separation of every human being from God:

O My God, My God, why have You abandoned Me?

91

He felt all our loneliness, all our sense of desertion and abandonment. All our deepest fears that, especially at the moment of death, can drown a soul in waves of despair.

And because He experienced all of this out of His infinite love for us – for each and every one of us, we have the blessed assurance that no one will ever face death alone.

In every hospital and ICU unit, every Nursing Home, every bed of suffering in America and around the world, where our fellow human beings are enduring pain and fear, where they are facing death, our Lord Jesus Christ is with them all.

In the deepest and most profound spiritual reality that a person can confront – the moment of their own death, our Lord is with them because He already died with all of us and for all of us two thousand years ago. He transcends time and space, just as He transcended death by His Mighty Resurrection!

This, my beloved Brothers and Sisters in Christ, is our greatest hope. For it leads not to extinction, not to some nothingness after we die. It leads to our own resurrection from the dead and life everlasting.

Yes, one day, we must all die; because we are mortal, made so by sin. But He is immortal, and His gift to us through the Resurrection is eternal life.[95]

May we always remember our Lord Jesus Christ's willing sacrifice of perfect love for us, and hold this promise of hope in our hearts, to attain now in this moment of anxiety and fear – and even death – the Holiest Pascha of our lifetimes.

Amen.

87   Mark 15:34.

88   Psalm 22:1 (LXX).

89   John 17:5, καὶ νῦν δόξασόν με σύ, πάτερ, παρὰ σεαυτῷ τῇ δόξῃ ᾗ εἶχον πρὸ τοῦ τὸν κόσμον εἶναι παρὰ σοί

90   The definition of the Council of Chalcedon (451).

91   Saint John Chrysostom, Homily 82 on the Gospel of Matthew.

92   Cf. Matthew 26:39.

93   Luke 22:44.

94   Cf. Romans 6:23.

95   Ibid.

22

Royal Hours and Vespers
of the Descent from the Cross

Holy and Great Friday

April 17, 2020

ARCHDIOCESE CHAPEL OF SAINT PAUL
NEW YORK, NEW YORK

Beloved Brothers and Sisters in Christ,

We have arrived at a grim, yet gentle moment in our challenging journey to Pascha. We have passed through the Matins of Holy Friday that we served last night – hearing the Twelve Gospels that tell the story of our Lord's love for us.

And we have just passed through the Great and Royal Hours of Holy Friday, that relive the Betrayal, Arrest, Trial, Torture, Crucifixion, and Death in the flesh of our Lord Jesus Christ.

We heard again the awesome Σήμερον Κρεμᾶται, that speaks of the One hanging on the Cross, Who suspended the earth in the midst of the waters.

Who receives a crown of thorns, though He is the King of the Angels.

Who is clothed in the purple of mockery, though He adorns the sky with the clouds.

Who is struck by His own creation, though He freed Adam in the Jordan.

Who is hammered through with nails, though He is the Bridegroom of the Church.

Who is pierced by a lance, though He is the Son of the Virgin.

In these moments when we recount Τὰ Πάθη Του – His Holy Passion, we can do nothing less than bow down and worship with body, mind, and soul; and implore Him to show us His Resurrection.

But in the μεταξύ of our Lord's dying and rising again, there is this three-day pause that commences with the Service we call Ἀποκαθήλωσις, the Descent of the Body of the Lord from the Cross.

It is a most grim and frightening moment, but one that has gentleness, loving-kindness, and deeply sorrowful care. The kind of care that only parents could give an only-begotten child at an untimely and unjust death.

Our Lord's earthly father, Joseph, was no longer alive. Therefore, another Joseph had to emerge from the shadows of fear, and serve Him as a father.

So it was that Joseph of Arimathea came forward, although he had much to lose. He was a rich man who gave his tomb to Jesus.[96] He was a member of the Sanhedrin who had not agreed with their actions against the Lord.[97] But he found the courage to go to Pilate, the Roman Procurator who had ordered the crucifixion of the Lord, and begged for His Body.

Here is love! Here is courage! Here is faith in a coming dawn when there is only darkness before your eyes!

Behold, none of the remaining Eleven Disciples showed such faith, such courage, or such love. They were in hiding, cowering for fear of exposure. They were afraid.

And it is true, my beloved Faithful, that fear is the opposite of love. It's not hatred. Hatred is a perverted and twisted form of love. This is why John, the Disciple of love, says: "Perfect love casts our fear."[98]

The miracle of this moment, when it took such bravery to take the naked, lifeless Body of the Lord down from the Cross, is love.

And that is why I say – for all its horror and grim sadness, there is yet a gentle, caring, and loving quality to this moment.

For those who pulled the nails out of His hands and feet,

Who lifted the thorny crown from His brow,

Who wiped the blood from His wounded head, His scourged back, His pierced side, His nailed hands and feet.

And, as we chant … σινδόνι καθαρᾷ εἰλήσας καὶ ἀρώμασιν, ἐν μνήματι καινῷ κηδεύσας ἀπέθετο … wrapped Him in a clean shroud, and laid Him in a new tomb.

If there is any lesson for us in this mystical moment today, it is that in the worst conditions, when all hope seems lost, it is love that will give us the courage to press on.

It is love that will steel our wills to do what is right, what is just, and what is needful.

It is love that will cast our fears away and overcome all our doubts.

We see it all around us in the doctors and nurses who love their fellow human beings more than they fear the coronavirus. We see it in the countless public servants who still do their often mundane jobs so that life can go on for the rest of us.

And I pray, that with the Lord's grace we will see this love in ourselves and share it with one another, for it is the bridge that crosses the abyss between death and life, between Hell and Heaven, and leads from Golgotha to the Empty Tomb on the glorious morning of the Resurrection.

Καλή Ἀνάστασῃ!

---

96   Cf. Isaiah 53:9.
97   Cf. Luke 23:51.
98   I John 4:18.

23

Service of the Lamentations at the Tomb

The Matins of Holy and Great Saturday

April 17, 2020

ARCHDIOCESE CHAPEL OF SAINT PAUL
NEW YORK, NEW YORK

My Beloved Christians,

Tonight – in our Churches with our clergy, and in our Home-Churches with all of you, we gather before the sacred *Epitaphios*, the image of our Lord Jesus Christ laid in the Tomb.

We come together to offer our love, our hymns, our songs of lamentation and praise, for they are yoked together tonight in a strange and profound way.

We mourn for the dead Christ, yet we glorify His abyss of love for us that endured the Cross.

We grieve with the Panagia for the loss of her only Son, yet we know that as the Son of God He hastens to the underworld to burst asunder the gates of Hades and harrow the depths of Hell.

We lament Him as He takes His Great Sabbath of Rest in the Tomb, yet we affirm that He will rise from the Tomb on the Third Day.

In these many hymns, and especially in the Ἐγκώμια that we chant with all our heart and soul, we pour forth to the King of Glory our adoration and our thankfulness for the great sacrifice He accomplished to save our souls.

This service is indeed the funeral service of our God, and this, as the Scripture says, is a σημεῖον ἀντιλεγόμενον, a "sign of contradiction."[99] How can we have a funeral for God? How can God die? The mystery of God's Incarnation, of the total yet sinless Humanity of the Lord, is a chasm that no human mind can bridge. Yet we believe it – it is the foundation of our Faith, and we know it to be true.

My beloved Christians, we assemble in the Spirit, in virtual space rather than physical, that we may reverence the greatness of God. And we contemplate how our worship can come together in the Spirit to strengthen us in this, our hour of need.

First, let us dedicate this Service of the Ἐγκώμια to all those who have perished as a result of the coronavirus. Let us make of this Funeral of the Lord their funeral, of which so many were deprived around the world. Let us remember them by name as you are able, and by intention for those that you do not know. Our combined prayers are able to console the living. And they can – in the eternal "Now" of God's presence – bring comfort to that moment of dying, when the body is most vulnerable and the soul needs protection as it journeys forth.

Second, let us consider how much this present separation can teach us. We feel disjointed from our usual routines, splintered from our relationships, and fragmented within our society. But if we examine our lives closely, this has always been the case. It's just that now we feel it so intensely.

Our lives have become like the valley of dry bones, as we read in the Prophesy of Ezekiel tonight. We are scattered, disordered, fearful, anxious, and weary from this plague that afflicts the world.

Our spirits are parched and thirst for the life that we once knew. Frustration and anger in the face of an invisible force that can bring death in a matter of days is understandable, but it cannot be the place where we take our stand!

From our hearts, with our minds, and deep within our spirits we must be like Ezekiel, stand and speak the word of the Lord. We must give flesh to the word of the Lord in our lives. This is what prophecy truly is. It's not predicting the future. It is speaking God's word in every aspect of our life, so that we become a living Scripture that any person could read.

And if we are willing to become prophets in and of our own lives, we will witness the valleys of dry bones, which are full of hopelessness, despair, and regret for better times – we will see them come alive again. Slowly, deliberately, the bones will come together, the sinews will grow, and our existence will literally flesh out in new and blessed ways. Because the Spirit of God, the Holy Breath of God, will infuse our lives, as we invoke His Presence.

This is the promise of this Funeral of Christ that we celebrate tonight. We do not consign the Prince of Life to corruption, to become only dry bones Himself.[100] And we do we not give up our Faith in the One Who breathes new life into us all.

There is always darkness before the dawn. And there is always death before Resurrection.

My beloved People of God. Take courage! Have hope! Hear the word of the Lord:

And you shall know that I am the Lord, when I have opened your graves, O My people, and brought you up out of your graves![101]

Καλή Ἀνάσταση!

---

99   Luke 2:34.
100 Cf. Psalm 15:10 (LXX).
101 Ezekiel 37:13.

24

Divine Liturgy of the First Resurrection

The Vespers of Holy and Great Saturday

April 18, 2020

Archdiocese Chapel of Saint Paul
New York, New York

My Beloved Christians,

Σιγησάτω πᾶσα σάρξ βροτεία, καὶ στήτω μετὰ φόβου καὶ τρόμου, καὶ μηδὲν γήϊνον ἐν ἑαυτῇ λογιζέσθω.

Let all mortal flesh keep silence, and stand with fear and trembling; and let it take no thought for any earthly thing.[102]

Indeed, my dear Brothers and Sisters in Christ, we keep silence and interior stillness in the presence of this profound mystery, the Sabbath of Rest of our Lord in the Tomb.

We hear the ancient prophecies of this day – there are fifteen by tradition – that were used in this Baptismal Liturgy. Today, the Catechumens went down into the Font of Rebirth, just as Christ descended into the grave and beyond, in order to be reborn.

For this Sabbath, this Seventh Day of the week is even greater than the Seventh Day on which God rested from the creation of the Cosmos.[103] On this Holy and Great Saturday, God the Son rested from His work of re-creating our human nature. In willingly dying upon the Cross, He made it possible for each and every human person to be reborn with Him by His Resurrection from the dead. He made it possible for our lives to be utterly transformed. He made it possible for us to live in the highest potential of our created form, as loving, merciful, compassionate, forgiving and altruistic persons.

And in taking His rest on the Seventh Day, the Lord Jesus fills all things with Himself, as is said in one of the final prayers of the *Proskomidi*:

Ἐν τάφῳ σωματικῶς, ἐν ᾅδου δὲ μετὰ ψυχῆς ὡς Θεός· ἐν Παραδείσῳ δὲ μετά λῃστοῦ, καὶ ἐν θρόνῳ ὑπῆρχες Χριστέ, μετὰ Πατρὸς καὶ Πνεύματος, πάντα πληρῶν ὁ ἀπερίγραπτος.

In the Tomb with Your Body, in Hades with Your soul as God, in Paradise with the Thief, and on the throne, O Christ, with the Father and the Spirit – You Who cannot be encompassed, fill all things.

In death He transcends every limitation of space and time. And by descending into the realm of the dead, He offers them the same eternal life that He offers us. No one is left behind.

In all the sacred Scripture that is read today, there are so many images and metaphors, so many similitudes and iconic narratives that manifest the truth of our Faith.

But perhaps, in this moment, when we are all struggling in the global pandemic, there is one that speaks directly to us. It is in the Prophecy of Daniel, when the Angel of the Lord descends into the

Fiery Furnace with the Three Holy Youths, and protects them from the burning fire.[104]

We see in the very same image the Incarnation and at the same time, the Descent into Hell. And for us, it is the image of the solidarity of God with us in this global pandemic. You see, there is no danger, no suffering, no sickness that we can experience, that God will not join. He is with us in every aspect of our Human experience except one … sin.

And by being present with us, even to the point of death and lying in a tomb, He redeems our human condition, in unseen and unforeseen ways. The Righteous Women with the Panagia, Joseph and Nikodemos, could not see the Lord's Descent and Conquest of Hell. They only saw the stone that was rolled before the entryway of the Tomb. But though the Garden where He was buried was shrouded in silence, in the netherworld of the dead there was a triumphant cry of the Angels of God who accompanied their Lord and King as He burst the gates of Hell asunder.

And so it is for us: what we see and what we hear is not the entire story. In the course of this pandemic, many lives will be lost and many lives will be saved, but God is with each and every one in their personal fiery furnace.

That is why we cry: Ἀνάστα ὁ Θεός! Arise O God! Because we know in our hearts that as He is risen from the dead, so shall it be for every one of us, who believe in His Holy Name, and live in His Holy Light. Amen.

Καλή Ἀνάσταση!

---

102 The Cherubic Hymn of Holy Saturday.
103 Cf. Genesis 2:2.
104 Cf. Daniel 3:49,50 (LXX).

25

Archiepiscopal Encyclical on the Great and Holy Pascha

April 19, 2020

To the Most Reverend Hierarchs, the Reverend Priests and Deacons, the Monks and Nuns, the Presidents and Members of the Parish Councils of the Greek Orthodox Communities, the Distinguished Archons of the Ecumenical Patriarchate, the Day, Afternoon, and Church Schools, the Philoptochos Sisterhoods, the Youth, the Hellenic Organizations, and the entire Greek Orthodox Family in America

My Beloved Christians,

Νῦν πάντα πεπλήρωται φωτός…

Now all things are filled with light… (Paschal Canon, Ode 2)

In this time of darkness: through the most difficult Lent in memory, through a radical reduction of our lives and livelihood, through the threat of sickness on an unprecedented scale, and through the grievous loss of family, friends, and neighbors taken from us too soon, we have finally arrived at the dawn.

Like the Myrrh-Bearing Women, going to the Tomb λίαν πρωὶ, ὄρθρου βαθέος – "very early in the morning, in the deep of the dawn"

– we are yet in the depths of a darkness from which we pray to be delivered. But we hold fast to the promise of this night:

Καὶ τὸ φῶς ἐν τῇ σκοτίᾳ φαίνει, καὶ ἡ σκοτία αὐτὸ οὐ κατέλαβεν.

And the light shines on in the darkness, never overcome by the darkness. (John 1:5)

Indeed, and in very truth, "Now all things are filled with light!" The Light of Christ, Who is Himself the Light of the world, can never be extinguished. It chases away the shadow of even the darkest soul, and it burns most brightly in the human heart, which with every beat sings praises to the Lord of Glory.

He fills the world with His Light, enlightening our souls through love, forgiveness, compassion and mercy. And if this year we cannot pass that light from candle to candle, we can still pass that same light from heart to heart. The holiest fire that burns without destroying is love, *for our God is a consuming fire* (Hebrews 12:29). Indeed, God loved the world so intensely that there was no suffering that He would not embrace in order to enfold us in His love. On His Precious and Life-Giving Cross, He showed us with one word that His Passover, His Pascha from death to life, would be the fulfillment for us all: Τετέλεσται! "It is accomplished!"

But now Christ is risen from the dead! Νυνὶ δὲ Χριστὸς ἐγήγερται ἐκ νεκρῶν! (I Cor. 15:20) He is the firstfruits of them that slept in death, and as Lord of both the living and the dead, He is the promise, the "Amen," of our future life in eternity.

Therefore, my beloved brothers and sisters, let us rejoice in the light of the Resurrection that shines across the Heavens, around the globe, and in our hearts. This dawn knows no horizon line; it shines even in the depths of hades.

Embrace the light with all your heart, soul, mind, and strength. Share it with everyone in gratitude and gentleness. Recognize its power to transform you and transfigure the world. And know, by faith, that the shadows we experience today are fleeting, cast by the Light Who is come upon us to dispel every darkness, and to raise us up with Him to everlasting light and life!

Χριστὸς Ἀνέστη! Ἀληθῶς Ἀνέστη! Christ is Risen! Truly He is Risen!

With paternal love in Christ Jesus,

† ELPIDOPHOROS
Archbishop of America

26

Archiepiscopal Message in *Kathimerini*
April 18, 2020

The pandemic that has shaken our planet to the core has also wounded the very heart of the Church: the Divine Liturgy, the gathering of the faithful, and our receiving Holy Communion. Especially during these days leading to Pascha, Christians are pained by these privations in this unsettling year. We are separated: from worshiping the Crucified One, from walking with the Epitaphios with a candle in hand, from receiving the Holy Light of the Resurrection, from receiving the Body and Blood of Christ. Nevertheless, I believe that the pandemic will not weaken the Church, rather it will strengthen it. And it will do so because it will draw our attention to the value of the Church's central message: the message of love, of solidarity, of the essential quality of the spirit. After all, in the course of history, our Church has always excelled in times when She and humanity itself have undergone hard trials. In such times, the name of God is glorified even more. Yes, our rituals may be temporarily altered and the ways we express our faith modified until we can come together again in our churches. But the ideals that motivate us and the values that inspire us, will inspire more and more people who are in the midst of yesterday's grief and their worry about today and tomorrow, and God's eternal mercy will redefine their lives.

The coronavirus cannot enslave the Church; rather it liberates Her. The Faithful may find themselves physically distant from our churches, but spiritually and mentally they are coming closer than ever to the Church and Her teaching. Today, they are more thirsty for prayer. They are learning to approach it in a new way, with the silence of a different mystagogy and the voice of their own soul, as they internalize the purpose of prayer and seek within themselves its theology. The exercise of our religious practices is not being threatened, but merely adapted for the time being, in response to the facts on the ground and in order to protect the supreme value of human life, the highest gift of God to man. Now we are closer to God. Now that we are unable to go to church and reverence His image, we turn within ourselves to behold it in our own hearts and souls.

Such reflection, through repentance, forgiveness, and confession, is part and parcel of the Church. And now, facing the challenge of dealing with the coronavirus, the whole of humanity is obliged to rethink its way of life, to reconsider priorities, to turn from a damaged materialistic "value" code to true and lasting values. The modern person of the Western World turned individualism into an ideology that identified happiness with success, wealth, and every form of materialism. He now realizes -- dramatically so – that there is no salvation for just one or the few, and that wealth is not always an absolute shield of protection. He now realizes that greed, exemplified by the destruction of the environment in the name of profit, can have unforeseen and uncontrollable effects that bring even worse disasters. He now realizes that he is not God, that he is not omnipotent. He now realizes that fear, pain, and death concern both the first and the last, and that calamity can happen to everyone without exception. The distinctions of this world - racial, religious, social, economic, class and all the others - "disappear" in the face of a common invisible enemy, which threatens all indiscriminately. He now realizes that each of us, all of us, are equal and equally valuable children of God.

He also realizes that those worthy of admiration are not the powerful, the glamorous, the "influencers," full of sound and fury. On the contrary, those worthy of our admiration are undetected by the radar of ephemeral publicity and glory; they are silent, invisible. They offer with selflessness and passion for the common good: doctors and nurses fighting every day in hospitals, researchers and scientists searching for treatments and vaccines, workers who ensure a basic regularity in our daily lives, cashiers and supermarket employees, food and beverage distributors, street cleaners, police and so many others who are far from home, out in the danger so that we can be in our homes and in safety.

My sadness for the thousands of my fellow human beings who are being severely tested and lost in America is the other side of the coin to my happy relief for what is happening in Greece, which has managed to avoid choosing between life and death for its people. I always knew that our motherland had great potential and could be a positive example for the whole world. And that is what is taking place. The Greek community in the United States looks proudly at its native soil and takes courage.

When we overcome this challenge, the time will come when each of us, and indeed all of us, collectively will answer the question of what we did, and who we were during the time of this pandemic. Much will change; we don't know how much or how exactly. But we do know that this notion of social distancing in a time of trial is now inscribed in our collective unconscious not as a punitive decision, but as another way of communicating, more silent, more internal. Today we realize more than ever how important our relationships with each other are, the value of contact, touch, and the physical expressions of

113

emotion. We realize how precious and unique everything we have is and more so, when we are temporarily forced to be separated from them. Indeed, the more solid and matter of fact we thought they were might be the reason we undervalued them. I hope that through this ordeal, we will learn to respect our relationships more, attributing to them the value they have beyond their self interest to us. I hope we will respect our life in the body more, and connect it with nature and the earth's ecosystems, the sacred creation of God that we must protect.

Then we, who call ourselves Christians, will be entitled to claim that we have respected science, which never conflicts with our faith, that we have followed its dictates, and that we have remained responsible and restrained, maintaining within our patience and composure, our serenity and spiritual practice, and our love and compassion for our fellow human beings. We did stay temporarily away from our churches to get closer to God. We stayed out of danger, putting health and life first for ourselves and for our fellow human beings, for the very people that God the Father sent His Son to die on the Cross. Out of love. For us to rise again. Καλή Ανάσταση!

27

Vespers of Agape

The Holy and Great Pascha

April 19, 2020

ARCHDIOCESE CHAPEL OF SAINT PAUL
NEW YORK, NEW YORK

My Beloved Christians,

Χριστὸς Ἀνέστη! Ἀληθῶς Ἀνέστη!

Christ is Risen! Truly He is Risen!

Δόξα τῇ ἁγίᾳ αὐτοῦ τριημέρῳ ἐγέρσει!

Glory to His Three-Day Resurrection!

With these glorious words, I greet each and every one of you in the joy of the Lord and the joy of this day. This truly is the Day that the Lord has made; let us rejoice together and be glad in it![105]

We have come through harsh and difficult days – the most challenging Lent in anyone's memory. And we have still arrived at the Holy Pascha of the Lord, for nothing could halt the Resurrection of Christ.

This is a sign for us, that even in the midst of this pandemic, we will pass over from death to life, from sickness to health, and from the current isolation to fellowship and communion again in the bonds of love and peace.

We know that on this Eve of the Resurrection, the Disciples were in hiding – καὶ τῶν θυρῶν κεκλεισμένων ὅπου ἦσαν οἱ μαθηταὶ συνηγμένοι διὰ τὸν φόβον – "and the doors were sealed shut where the Disciples had gathered because of fear…."

The Disciples feared the Judeans, those who had called out "Crucify Him!" We are also behind closed doors, but not merely from fear of the coronavirus. In fact, we are not hiding at all. We are sheltering for the sake of our own health, and for the health and safety of our fellow human beings.

But just like the Disciples, when we least expect it, our Risen Lord comes to us, granting us His peace. To the Disciples, He passed through the locked doors and the solid walls; to us, He enters the deepest recesses of our hearts and instills in us His peace that surpasses every human understanding.[106]

My beloved Brothers and Sisters in the Risen Christ, I know that this is not an easy time to celebrate the Holy Pascha – without our traditional festal meals and gatherings. But the Resurrection is so much more than an occasion for the celebration of an ancient event. It is the daily rising in our hearts of the Sun of Righteousness, Who bears healing in His wings.[107]

There will always be a part of us – the "Thomas particle" I would call it – that will always doubt the reality and the efficacy of believing. Just as when his fellow Disciples told him that they had seen the Lord, Thomas replied:

"Unless I see in His hands the mark of the nails, and unless I put my finger into the wound of the nails, and I unless I stick my hand into His side, I will never believe!"[108]

His words are as full of pain and anger as they are of doubt and disbelief. He is fixated on the Passion and the Death, because he cannot comprehend how such suffering and sacrifice could emerge in triumph. Let us not forget that he was in the same kind of isolation that many of us are today. The Scripture reports that he was not with the other Disciples when Jesus appeared to them.[109]

My dear friends, the same is true for many of us – maybe all of us. There is a part of us that cannot see our way through the pandemic, and we share in the pain and outrage of Thomas.

But fear not. Christ will come to you, just as He came to Thomas, "after eight days,"[110] and you will know from that encounter that God is real, that Heaven is real, and that Christ is truly risen from the dead, trampling down death by death, and to those in the tombs bestowing life!

Χριστὸς Ἀνέστη! Ἀληθῶς Ἀνέστη!

---

105 Psalm 117:24 (LXX).
106 Cf. Philippians 4:7.
107 Cf. Malachi 4:2.
108 John 20:25.
109 John 20:24.
110 John 20:26.

28

Great Vespers of
Saint George the Trophy-Bearer

April 22, 2020

SAINT GEORGE – SAINT DEMETRIOS
GREEK ORTHODOX CHURCH
NEW YORK, NEW YORK

My Beloved Brothers and Sisters in the Risen Christ,

Χριστὸς Ἀνέστη! Ἀληθῶς Ἀνέστη!

Christ is Risen! Truly He is Risen!

What a joy it is to be with you in this historic and beautiful parish of Saint George and Saint Demetrios, the two warrior Saints who are in reality great healers and peacemakers. Indeed, as the Lord said:

Μακάριοι οἱ εἰρηνοποιοί, ὅτι αὐτοὶ υἱοὶ Θεοῦ κληθήσονται.

Blessed are the peacemakers, for they shall be called the sons of God.[111]

Of these "sons of God," this evening we welcome the feast of the Great-Martyr and Trophy-Bearer George – whose fame extends throughout the ages and around the world.

This Bright Week, because the day of his Feast, April 23rd, falls after the Holy Pascha, we retain the date of his Feast. But it is significant to note that whenever April 23rd falls before the Holy Pascha – during Lent or Holy Week – the celebration of Saint George is moved to Bright Monday, because this Holy Great-Martyr is considered so important by the Church, that his Feast should not be diminished in any way.

As we chant in his Apolytikion, he is "τῶν αἰχμαλώτων ἐλευθερωτής, τῶν πτωχῶν ὑπερασπιστής, τῶν ἀσθενούντων ἰατρός" – "the one who sets the captives free, the defender of those in poverty, and the physician of those facing infirmity."

Therefore, we come to the Trophy-Bearer George in our moment of need:

When we are facing the captivity of isolation and confinement that is necessary to protect our health and the safety of others;

When we are facing impoverishment due to the stranglehold on our economy due to the pandemic;

And when we are facing the challenge of sickness ourselves, and of those that we love.

We come to Saint George with our prayers and supplications, asking him, as he was also the Champion of Kings – Βασιλέων Ὑπέρμαχος – to be our Champion in this time of need and distress.

We pray that his love for Christ – a love that compelled him to accept a Passion and Holy Week of his very own – pour forth upon us who are the Body of Christ, His Holy Bride and Church.

We pray that as a true husbandman of the earth – the very meaning of his name, Γεώργιος – he will use all his care, all his skill, all his

120

power of intercessory prayer, to set creation aright, and end this global pandemic.

We pray that together with his brother in arms, Saint Demetrios, whose name is glorified in this parish along with his own, they will together fight for us in every way, to deliver us from harm.

As is chanted in the Canon of the day:

Δημήτριε Μάρτυς, σὺν Γεωργίῳ τῷ κλεινῷ· ἀγαθοὶ γὰρ οἱ δύο, μηδαμῶς ἐλλίπητε, τόνδε τὸν χῶρον φρουροῦντες ἀεί, καὶ πειρασμῶν, ὅλας μυριάδας, μετακινοῦντες ἀμφότεροι.

O Martyr Demetrios, with the famed George, truly both are blessed, in nothing lacking, always keeping watch over this earth, and they both cast away the myriads of our trials.[112]

May it always be so!
Χριστὸς Ἀνέστη! Ἀληθῶς Ἀνέστη!

---

111 Matthew 5:9.
112 Canon One, Ode Nine of the Great-Martyr.

29

Great Vespers
of the Life-Giving Fountain
April 23, 2020

Zoodohos Peghe Greek Orthodox Church
The Bronx, New York

Beloved Brothers and Sisters in the Risen Christ,

Χριστὸς Ἀνέστη! Ἀληθῶς Ἀνέστη!

Christ is Risen! Truly He is Risen!

This evening we return to the source, the wellspring, the fountain of our blessings and our joy: the Mother of God. As we sing in the Liturgies of this Paschal Season:

Ἐν Ἐκκλησίαις εὐλογεῖτε τὸν Θεόν, Κύριον ἐκ πηγῶν Ἰσραήλ.

In the Churches bless God, the Lord from the wellsprings of Israel.[113]

She is indeed our blessing from God, for her womb was the wellspring of the Heavenly blessing of the Incarnate God, Who has shown her to be a fountain of healing for the whole world.

This fountain of love and marvels is exemplified by the most famous Church of the Life-Giving Spring in the Μπαλουκλί quarter of the Queen of Cities, Constantinople. Μπαλουκλί means "fish" in Turkish language, because fish live in the pool of fresh water that continues to flow to this day. Over fifteen hundred years ago, a Church was built over the ἁγίασμα, over the sacred spring that flows with miracles. Like the Pool of Siloam – which we will celebrate on the Sixth Sunday of Pascha, the Ζωοδόχος Πηγή granted sight to the blind, and was revealed as a source of healing and grace.

As a sign of the healing in this Πηγή, a hospital was built just a short distance away to serve the Greek Orthodox Community. Its ministry is part of our Ecumenical Patriarchate's operations in Constantinople that bring comfort and therapies to the faithful there, who are in the same situation as we are in this global pandemic. In fact, the Hospital is open to all people, and is renown as one of the best in the City.

Think of it! For fifteen hundred years the Virgin has graced the people with her healing touch – whether through the many miracles that come from the Πηγή, or from the medical staff who sacrificially serve in Her name. In either case, we witness the love of God, a love that flows like the waters of the Life-Giving Fountain.

In the services of this Feast, we acclaim the Virgin:

Μάννα Σιλωάμ, καὶ Στοὰν Σολομῶντος
Πηγὴν Κόρη σὴν ἐμφανῶς πᾶς τις βλέπει.

The Manna, Siloam, and the Stoa of Solomon,
are to all men manifestly apparent in thy Spring, O Maiden.[114]

We call the Virgin "Manna," the "Bread of the Angels"[115] because she was revealed by Gabriel, the Prince of the Angels, to be the source of the human nature, the Body of our Lord.[116] As the Apostle Paul points out, she is the source of the humanity of our Lord.[117]

But we also name her "Siloam," after the famous Pool in Jerusalem where the Lord healed the Man Born Blind.[118] Indeed, because the Πηγή at Μπαλουκλί was first revealed by the healing of a blind man, she becomes the living pool of healing and mercies.

And we call her the Stoa, the Portico of Solomon, because she is the image of the Church, the Bride of Christ. It was in the Stoa, this portion of the rebuilt Temple of Solomon, that the Disciples gathered after the Ascension of the Lord, as is recorded in the Book of Acts. There, they manifested the nature of the Church – miraculous ways of being, unity and harmony, and above all worship of the One True God.

> *And many signs and wonders were done among the people through the hands of the Apostles. And they were all with one accord in the Stoa of Solomon.*[119]

Therefore, we give thanks for the Mother of God – whose heart is a fountain of healing, whose body is the source of the Bread of Heaven Himself, and whose life is the story of the Church. May we always be united to Her in prayer, in supplication, and above all, love.

Χριστὸς Ἀνέστη! Ἀληθῶς Ἀνέστη!

---

113 Eisodikon of Pascha, Psalm 67:27 (LXX).
114 Verses of the Synaxarion of the Matins of the Life-Giving Fountain.
115 Psalm 77:28.
116 Luke 1:35.
117 Cf. Galatians 4:4.
118 John 9:1-7.
119 Acts 5:12.

30

Sunday of Thomas

April 26, 2020

HOLY RESURRECTION GREEK ORTHODOX CHURCH
BROOKVILLE, NEW YORK

Brothers and Sisters in the Risen Christ,

Χριστὸς Ἀνέστη! Ἀληθῶς Ἀνέστη!

Christ is Risen! Truly He is Risen!

And though the doors were sealed shut – καὶ τῶν θυρῶν κεκλεισμένων, the Lord appeared.

Though the doors were sealed shut because of fear, the Lord appeared, and granted peace.

Though the doors were sealed shut, the Lord appeared, and faith was renewed.

We are gathered yet again on the Eighth Day after the Resurrection, most of us sealed shut in our homes, and the fear of the pandemic still prevailing in our world. And we are gathered this morning in the Church of the Resurrection, here in Brookville, New York, in order to continue our affirmation of the Anastasis, of the newness of life

FAITH IN THE TIME OF COVID-19

that commenced two thousand years ago, and extends to this day and to this hour.

Indeed, one could say that the Day of Resurrection – the First Day of the Week after the Sabbath of God's rest from His labors of salvation on our behalf – is indeed the Beginning of the Eighth Day of Creation;

The Eighth Day that is the unwaning day of His Kingdom;[120]

The Eighth Day that is mirrored in today's Feast that we call Thomas Sunday.

We all know the story. Thomas was not present with the other Disciples on the evening of Pascha, one week ago, when the Lord appeared to them miraculously within the locked room. And when the Disciples told Thomas later on about the Resurrection appearance of the Lord, Thomas replied:

Unless I see in His hands the mark of the nails, and unless I put my finger into the wound of the nails, and I unless I stick my hand into His side, I will never believe![121]

Thomas is defiant, adamant, even mocking. A far cry from his declaration just a few weeks prior when the Lord said he was returning to Bethany for the dead Lazaros. Then Thomas exclaimed, *"Let us also go, that we may die with Him!"*[122]

You see, Thomas, like so any of the other Disciples at different times, had a misplaced enthusiasm for the Lord's ministry and miracles. He had witnessed so many marvels, but had not as yet understood their meaning.

Therefore, in the face of the loss of his Master and Lord, he becomes aggressive and obstinate, frustrated at the suggestion that Christ might indeed be risen from the dead. He doubts his brothers, because he doubts himself, and thus we know him as, "Doubting Thomas."

It is too easy for us to judge Thomas, especially in his moment of loss and weakness. Truly, we are not so different from him in our current circumstances of pain, loss, and frustration. We have all known times in our lives when we felt strong in our faith, that we could even confront our own death with courage and confidence. But then a Holy Week happens like the one we just experienced, and all the pillars on which we have leaned our whole lives come crashing down. And we are like Thomas.

We are hurt.

We are angry.

And we demand proof that what we believe is real.

My beloved Christians, there are so many lessons that we can learn from Thomas; he has much to teach us.

Thomas was not with the other Disciples when the Lord appeared, and although the other Ten affirmed the Resurrection to him, he would not accept their testimony. Perhaps he was angry that he had not been included in that vision of the Lord. He had once been so willing to go all the way, even to the point of death. Perhaps now he was embarrassed by his reactions to the death of his Master and Lord, and was emotionally cut off from his brothers. He was alone and isolated.

This is what can easily happen to us in these days of the pandemic and the social distancing we are all doing now, for the sake of our own health and that of others.

We are shut off from our brothers and sisters in Christ. And even though I and your clergy continue to celebrate, we feel the same isolation and loneliness that you do, because we are cut off from you.

But there is Good News; though the doors are sealed shut – τῶν θυρῶν κεκλεισμένων,

the Lord appears;

the Lord grants peace;

the Lord is risen from the dead, trampling down death by death, and He grants unto us eternal life.

He will come to us in our isolation, in our loneliness, in our limitations, and He will manifest to us the miracle of eternal life, just as He did to Thomas. To each of us, in the Eighth Day of the Resurrection, He will invite us to come close to Him, to experience Him, as He did to Thomas:

> *After eight days, the Disciples were again assembled inside, and this time, Thomas was with them. Though the doors were sealed shut, Jesus came and stood in their midst and said, "Peace be unto you." Then Jesus addressed Thomas, "Bring your finger here and probe My hands. And take your hand and put it into My side. Doubt no more. Believe!" Thomas cried out to Him, "My Lord and my God!"*[123]

In this moment of profound challenge from the Lord, Thomas is reunited with his brothers. He lets go of his anger, his resentment, his shame. His confession is the greatest affirmation of Christ in the Gospels. Jesus Christ is both Lord and God! But hear how the Lord receives his worship and what He says to us:

> *Because you have seen Me, is it only now you believe? Blessed are those who have seen nothing, and yet they believe!*[124]

If you have not seen, you are blessed. If you have not experienced, you can believe. And if we cannot join together in person, we can do so in spirit, and still be the one community, the one Body, the one

Church of our Lord Jesus Christ, Who is alive, dead though He was, and is alive forevermore![125]

Χριστὸς Ἀνέστη! Ἀληθῶς Ἀνέστη!

---

120 Cf. the Ninth Ode of Pascha, "ἐν τῇ ἀνεσπέρῳ ἡμέρᾳ τῆς βασιλείας σου."

121 John 20:25.

122 John 11:6.

123 John 20:26-28.

124 John 20:29.

125 Revelation 1:18.

31

Sunday of the Myrrh-Bearing Women

May 3, 2020

HOLY TRINITY GREEK ORTHODOX CHURCH
NEW ROCHELLE, NEW YORK

Brothers and Sisters in Christ,

Χριστὸς Ἀνέστη! Ἀληθῶς Ἀνέστη!

Christ is Risen! Truly He is Risen!

I have one question for all of us this morning. One question, and one question alone.

Τίς ἀποκυλίσει ἡμῖν τὸν λίθον;

Who will roll away the stone for us?[126]

Who will roll away the sorrow of these times, which have shut us in living tombs of isolation and loneliness?

Who will roll away the angst, the worry, and the fear that imprison our minds and hearts day to day?

Who will roll away the burden, the onus, the pressure of the needs we have to meet and the families we have to support?

My Beloved Christians of the Holy Trinity Church in New Rochelle, our courageous parish at one of the early epicenters of the Pandemic, and all of you joining by virtual means, the question is: "Who will roll away the stone for us?"

The Faithful Myrrh-Bearers arrived at the Tomb in the deep dawn, to complete their mission of anointing the Body of the Lord Jesus Christ in accordance with the prevailing Jewish custom, but they did not prevail, for He had risen from the dead.

They were led by Mary Magdalene, from whom Christ had cast out seven demons. There was Salome, a daughter of Saint Joseph the Betrothed. Salome was the wife of the fisherman Zebedee and the mother of the Disciples, John the Evangelist and James. There was Joanna, the wife of Chuza, who was the steward of King Herod's household. There was Susanna, and Mary and Martha, the sisters of Lazarus. And there was Mary, the wife of Cleopas who encountered the Risen Lord on the Road to Emmaus.

The Women Disciples of the Lord were many, and they demonstrated a faith and commitment to Him in His earthly life that His Disciples could not.

Last Sunday, we witnessed the fear of the Disciples, hiding in the Upper Room behind locked doors, afraid of the Temple Authorities. And we saw how the Lord transformed their fear into peace, and the disbelief of Thomas into faith.

Today, we behold the devotion of the Myrrh-Bearers, whose love is mirrored by that of Nikodemos and Joseph of Arimathea, for together they took down the Precious Body of the Lord from the Cross, wrapped It in linen with spices, and laid It in the Tomb.

But they did not realize that even in death, the Body of the Lord was life-giving. For the Logos of God was never separated from His human soul or His human body.

They did not realize that He would not be inside the Tomb, waiting to be anointed, since His anointing had been accomplished before His Passion.

Indeed, my beloved Christians, they worried about the stone, for they did not as yet understand that:

> … *neither death nor life, nor Angels, nor Principalities nor Powers, nor things present, nor things future, nor height, nor depth, nor any other created thing will be able to separate us from the love of God that is in Christ Jesus, our Lord!*[127]

Not anything – certainly, not a stone! So what is the answer to our question today?

Perhaps our question is not phrased correctly. It is not: "Who will roll away the stone?" It is: "Why is the stone already rolled away?"

It is not about the weight of our grief, our isolation, our sadness, our fears, and our suffering. These are unavoidable; but we are not called not to focus on this impossible weight.

My dear Brothers and Sisters, the stone was rolled away not to let the Lord out, but to let us in.

There is only one way to the Resurrection, and it is through the Cross, through the Tomb, through following our Lord Jesus Christ all the way to the end. It is when we choose to enter into the full experience of the Lord's Θεανθρωπότης, His God-Manhood, that we begin to understand what it is to die to ourselves and to live to Him.

What it is to live for others;

To live for love, for mercy, for compassion, and forgiveness;

To choose the good of everyone else above our own.

This is dying before you die, as the Monks of Mount Athos know so well:

Ἄν πεθάνεις πρὶν πεθάνεις,
Δὲν θὰ πεθάνεις ὅταν πεθάνεις.

If you die before you die,
You will not die when you die.[128]

It is a willing choice, the same choice that led our Lord to die for us on the Cross. He willingly chose to die, as the Virgin so lovingly laments in the Holy Friday Homily of St. Symeon Metaphrastes:

So now let Your head sleep, my beloved Son, and let Your hands and Your feet rest. Others bow their heads in death, but not before they give up the spirit. But You bowed Your head, commanding death to come; only then did You give over Your spirit.[129]

Therefore, my beloved Christians, even in the midst of the suffering and hardship that surrounds us daily, let us cast our cares upon the Lord for He cares for us.[130]

The stone will be moved – even if God must send His Angels from heaven to do so!

And let us enter the Empty Tomb, a sure sign of the Resurrection and life eternal, that we may embrace a life of self-sacrifice, of altruism, of empathy, of compassion and above all love.

Then we may join those Myrrh-Bearers – those Apostles to the Apostles – and run to announce the glad tidings that:

Ἠγέρθη ὁ Κύριος ὄντως!

The Lord is risen indeed![131]

Χριστὸς Ἀνέστη! Ἀληθῶς Ἀνέστη!

126 Mark 16:3.
127 Romans 8:38,39.
128 Inscription at St. Paul's Monastery on Mount Athos.
129 Cf. John 19:30. On the Lament of the All-Holy Theotokos When She
      Embraced the Precious Body of our Lord Jesus, Saint Symeon the
      Metaphrast, Archbishop of Thessaloniki (P.G. 114, 217A)
130 Cf. I Peter 5:7.
131 Luke 24:34.